For BOYS ONLY

For BOYS ONLY

The Doctor Discusses the Mysteries of Manhood

DR. FRANK HOWARD RICHARDSON

HOW BOOKS
Cincinnati, Ohio
www.howdesign.com

 Published by HOW Books, an imprint of F+W Publications, Inc., 4700 East Galbraith Road, Cincinnati, Ohio 45236. (800) 289-0963. First edition.

For more fine books from F+W Publications, visit www.fwbookstore.com.

11 10 09 08 07 5 4 3 2 1

Distributed in Canada by Fraser Direct, 100 Armstrong Avenue, Georgetown, Ontario, Canada L7G 5S4, Tel: (905) 877-4411. Distributed in the U.K. and Europe by David & Charles, Brunel House, Newton Abbot, Devon, TQ12 4PU, England, Tel: (+44) 1626 323200, Fax: (+44) 1626 323319, E-mail: postmaster@davidandcharles.co.uk. Distributed in Australia by Capricorn Link, P.O. Box 704, Windsor, NSW 2756 Australia, Tel: (02) 4577-3555.

Library of Congress Cataloging-in-Publication Data

Richardson, Frank Howard, 1882-

For boys only : the doctor discusses the mysteries of manhood; and, For girls only : the doctor discusses the mysteries of womanhood / Frank Howard Richardson.

p. cm.

ISBN 978-1-60061-069-1 (pbk. : alk. paper)

1. Sex instruction for boys. 2. Sex instruction for girls. I. Richardson, Frank Howard, 1882- For girls only. II. Title. III. Title: For girls only.

HQ41.R485 2007

612.6--dc22 2007034837

Edited by Amy Schell

Designed by Grace Ring

Illustrated by Greg Nock

fw

F+W PUBLICATIONS, INC.

ABOUT THE AUTHOR

Dr. Frank Howard Richardson was educated in the United States (Cornell University) and in Europe (Vienna and Berlin). He was a pediatrician certified by the American Board of Pediatrics, and was a member of the American Academy of Pediatrics, The American College of Physicians, the Southern Medical Association and the American Medical Association. He was a lecturer and well-known writer, having contributed to leading medical journals and popular magazines. He is the author of ten books: *For Boys Only, For Girls Only, Simplifying Motherhood, Parenthood and the Newer Psychology, Rebuilding the Child, The Nervous Child and His Parents, The Pre-School Child and His Posture* (with Winifred J. Hearn), *Feeding Our Children, Letters From a Doctor to Expectant Parents*, and *The Nursing Mother: A Handbook on Breast Feeding*. He was also the father of two daughters and three sons.

Table of

CONTENTS

FOREWORD

When I was about five years old, my mother sat me down on the end of her bed and tried to explain "the birds and the bees" in terms that I'd understand. What I came away with was that a mommy and a daddy climbed into bed and went to sleep. Sometime during the night, tiny sperm would march out of the daddy (I wasn't sure from where), cross the bed and climb into the mommy. Somehow the sperm would find an egg, break into it and turn it into a baby.

It wasn't until she gave me a book called *Where Did I Come From*, a few years later, that I finally began to understand how it really works. The book included a cartoon drawing of a chubby couple in bed. I'm pretty sure the daddy was on top. "Oh," I said, as a light bulb went on in my head, "that makes much more sense than tiny sperm walking across a huge bed."

When I was maybe eight years old, my mother presented me with another book by the same author called *What's Happening to Me?*, which explained the mysteries of puberty. I remember looking at a drawing of a girl examining her growing chest and peeking down my own shirt to see what was going on down there.

I was young enough when my parents decided I should learn about the facts of life, that I took it rather seriously. If they'd waited a few more years, I would have been embarrassed by the whole thing. After that, the topic wasn't raised again until I went to college.

During the long drive to freshman orientation, my father tried to tell me something important. "You know, you'll want to be careful. If you go to parties and there's drinking, you should make sure not to get too drunk and stick with your friends. You know, don't go anywhere alone."

I wasn't quite sure what he was trying to say, besides, "Don't get drunk." During the orientation, one of the campus safety officers addressed the issue of date rape. My father leaned over and whispered, "That's what I was talking about."

"Really, could have fooled me," I thought to myself.

But my dad was certainly not alone in his inability to talk frankly about sex with me, which is why every generation has its own facts-of-life handbook that parents can give to their kids to avoid the awkward conversation (but still feel like they're doing a good job).

In fact, my mother once showed me the book that my grandmother had given her when she was about twelve years old. The small white pamphlet included lovely line illustrations and ridiculous advice like: Don't shower during menstruation, as you might catch a chill. And don't over-exert yourself with activities like swimming or horseback riding.

So when I came across a book called *For Boys Only: The Doctor Discusses the Mysteries of Manhood* in a dusty used bookstore, I happily paid a dollar for it and took my treasure home to peruse. First published in 1952, *For Boys Only* presents sex ed, health and dating advice in the form of a story. "Real" boys talk about girls and ask questions of a trusted local doctor who answers them frankly. I have one word for you: hilarious.

The book's back cover included a mention of another title called *For Girls Only* and I immediately knew I had to find that book, too. Luckily, we live in the era of eBay, and it only took me a few tries to track down a copy. True to form, it was just as side-splittingly funny as the boys book.

As I read through both books (and marked my favorite passages), I started to wonder if the teen-agers of the 1950s found these books just as amusing as I did...

The year is 1952. You're sitting on your bed sorting through your baseball card collection when your father appears in the doorway. "So sport," he says, because he often calls you sport when he's trying to speak *your language*. "I've got something for you."

You glance up to see that your father is holding a slim volume and gingerly handing it to you. "So, if you have any questions about girls or anything like that, your mother got this book from her friend Mrs. Whitman, who says it helped her son with the girls and other growing-up problems."

"Sure, Pop," you say, taking the book and tossing it to one end of your bed.

But I could just as easily imagine the same thing happening in 1975.

You're sitting on your bed sorting through your record collection. "So man," your father says, appearing in your doorway, "I've got a little something here for you. I think your Ma picked it up at a swap meet. Anyway, she digs it and thinks it might help you with the ladies and all that puberty stuff.

Or 2008, as you're sitting on your bed playing with your Wii (of the Nintendo variety). "So homie," your father says, even though he doesn't exactly know what that means. "Your Mom bought this for you at the airport. She had a nasty layover in Atlanta, but I guess she read it and thinks it will help you understand women and yourself."

Eventually, you'd pick up the book and flip through the pages. A few fun words like *sex, breasts* and *erection* would stand out and you'd start to read. But once you'd gotten through a few chapters, you'd begin to realize that while the book offered a few clues about the impending changes of puberty, it revealed much more about your parents and what their generation believed about sex and growing up.

And no matter what year it was, you'd know in your heart that they didn't have a clue.

So without further ado, we present in its entirety: *For Boys Only—The Doctor Discusses the Mysteries of Manhood.*

Enjoy!
Megan Lane Patrick
Editor

Chapter 1

IT'S A WRECK!

The siren wailed at a high pitch. And down the pike raced the wrecker, closely followed by an ambulance. They stopped, with shrieking brakes, just as Jack and the doctor reached the scene of the accident. The crowd, already milling round two jammed hulks that just minutes before had been shiny new sedans, stood aside to open up a passage for the doctor's car. As he stopped he saw two highway patrolmen dragging the apparently lifeless form of a fifteen-year-old boy from the driver's seat of one of the cars.

Jack, who does odd jobs for the doctor, was finishing his daily chore of sweeping the office sidewalk when a phone call had summoned the doctor to an accident a half mile out of town. Snatching up his emergency bag and calling "Hop in, Jack, if you want to come along," the doctor had jumped into his coupé, stepped on the starter, jammed the accelerator down to the floor, and they were off, swinging into the highway just behind the ambulance. Now, leaving the car, he pushed his way through the crowd that clustered round the unconscious form of the young driver, then asked everyone to stand back so as to give the boy some air.

After a brief but thorough going over, during which he examined the lad's eye reflexes and moved his arms, legs and body very gently to make sure there were no broken bones, the doctor rose to his feet. "He has a slight concussion, but probably no brain injury, luckily for him. Get him into the ambulance, and take him home and put him to bed. I'll come by and see him again in a few minutes, just as soon as I'm through here," and he turned to look over any other occupants of the wrecked cars that might need his help.

"Harry's a lucky boy," said the doctor next morning, as he finished his examination and pronounced the lad OK. He had found him sitting up and feeling fine, apparently none the worse for his adventure of the day before.

"Oh, good morning, Mr. Taylor," he nodded to Harry's father who had entered the room as he was leaving. "How that son of yours escaped from that head-on crash with nothing more serious than a temporary concussion and a few scratches is more than I can understand or explain. He's a very lucky lad, indeed."

Mr. Taylor interrupted angrily: "Lucky? *I* don't see anything lucky about it. That's the second brand new car he's wrecked, and he has had a half dozen very close squeaks. And invariably it's been because of some road hog who had no right to try to pass him. Each time he's tried to show them they couldn't get ahead of *him*. You can see what he has showed them–and showed me, too! I call it the worst kind of luck–though I can't blame him for being angry and trying to teach them a lesson." The baffled father grunted something under his breath that sounded very much like an oath, uncertain who to blame most–his reckless son, or the irresponsible motorists who had tempted the boy to take these ill-fated chances. Meanwhile, Harry, who up till then had been chatting pleasantly enough with the doctor, gave his father a look as black as a thundercloud. Noticing it, the doctor turned toward the bed.

"Your dad and I are both wrong, Harry–I for saying you were lucky, and he for blaming your bad luck for your troubles. It's not your bad luck that makes you wreck your dad's cars–it's losing your temper like a dumb adolescent, instead of acting like a man and letting other drivers kill themselves instead of ruining you."

"Mr. Taylor, if you'll forgive me for offering some advice you haven't asked me for, it's partly your fault for agreeing with Harry when he tries to spite these other drivers. Instead of explaining to him by quiet reasoning how foolish it is to try to assert his rights, you just scold him a bit and then let him go ahead and wreck another car. If he can't control *himself*, he's not old enough to try to drive a car that he can't control."

By this time Mr. Taylor looked pretty much like a thundercloud, too, but then he broke in with a short laugh:

"You're his doctor. If it's just adolescence that's ailing him, why don't you teach him how to manage it and control himself?"

"I'll do better than that. We're going to have a discussion down at school this week and we'll talk about driving cars and getting along with fathers, too, before we get through. I'll be looking for you, Harry," and the door closed behind him.

Chapter 2

I'LL BE THERE

It was just a few minutes before time for the school football game to begin when Jack knocked at the doctor's door, then came in rather bashfully. "Mother wants me to get something from you to cure these pimples that have been bothering me. I don't see why it is that so many of the fellows in my class have this messy skin trouble. Some of them aren't so bad, but others are much worse than I am, with big red bumps and boils that have to be lanced. What causes it, anyway, doctor?"

"That's quite a long story, Jack. I'm sure you'd be interested in it, and I'd love to talk to you about it. It opens up something I'm quite sure every boy wants to know about. Strangely enough, it has to do with the very thing I was talking to your friend Harry about yesterday. I wish we had time to talk about it now, but we haven't. But I'm going ... "

"Yeah, I saw Harry today, and he tells me that Prof has asked you to come to school and talk to us about some of the things that puzzle us, and that we can't find answers to. Prof says you do this every year. I'd sure like to hear what goes on there."

"That's right. I talk to the fellows for a while, and then they pop any questions at me they want to, and I try my best to answer them. Some of them are really humdingers with no holds barred. But right now you are on your way to the game, and I've got some calls to make.

"Save up your questions and tell any of the fellows you see to do the same. We always have a big time at these parties. After the general questions are over and chapel is dismissed, anyone is free to come down to the front and ask me anything he wants to, about any personal matter he might not like to have talked about in front of the whole school."

"Gee, that sounds great," said Jack. "I sure want to be there. And I'll bet you *will* get some humdingers, from what I've heard some of the fellows say when no one's around," and he grinned in anticipation of seeing the doctor squirm.

"So long, then, Jack. I'll be seeing you." And the doctor turned back into the house. As Jack hurried along the street, he was already wondering what questions he'd be hearing, and what he himself might ask, when the doctor came to school within the next few days.

Chapter 3

FROM BOY TO MAN

One day, the following week, the doctor appeared on the chapel platform and began his talk:

"Prof has asked me to come here this morning and talk with you about some of the things fellows talk about when older people are not around because they know folks aren't supposed to discuss such matters. But, as you can imagine, a doctor gets all kinds of questions thrown at him. He has so many different sorts that he gets used to being surprised, and nothing fazes him. It's my business to try to help people, not to judge them or criticize them.

"This morning, after I've told you some of the things I know all of you have been wondering and talking about, I'm going to let you ask me anything you want to. We won't have any kid stuff, like giggling and snickering when some fellow asks something you don't usually hear talked about out in the open. Let's really find out some things we'd like to know about this morning.

"Now, some of you may think you know just the person who can tell you everything along this line you need to know. You think it's the big guy in the class ahead of you who's 'been around' and is quite sure he knows all the answers. He may like to sound off and show you how wise he is, but don't let him fool you. He doesn't know much more about these things than you do. What's worse, a lot of what he knows just isn't so!

"So give him a brush-off when he tries to impress you with how much he knows, and by telling you how innocent and green you are. It will be much better to rely on someone who really knows and can give you straight answers.

"I'm going to try to be that person this morning, or any other time you may care to come to me and ask me something. If you stump me with something, I'll find somebody who knows the answer and send you to him, or bring his answer back to you.

"So now, let's go.

"Probably every fellow here this morning has wondered why it is that somewhere around the age that you are now, certain changes begin to take place in your body that are different from anything you've ever known before. Your voice begins to go haywire every once in a while when you are singing, and even at especially important and sometimes very embarrassing times when you're talking.

"Then, too, your skin may start showing blackheads–those ugly little black dots that come out when you squeeze them, followed by a little white waxy stuff. Keeping your face clean doesn't prevent them coming, either. Squeezing blackheads sometimes causes infection, and they turn first into red bumps and then into painful boils. Your skin, that you never used to

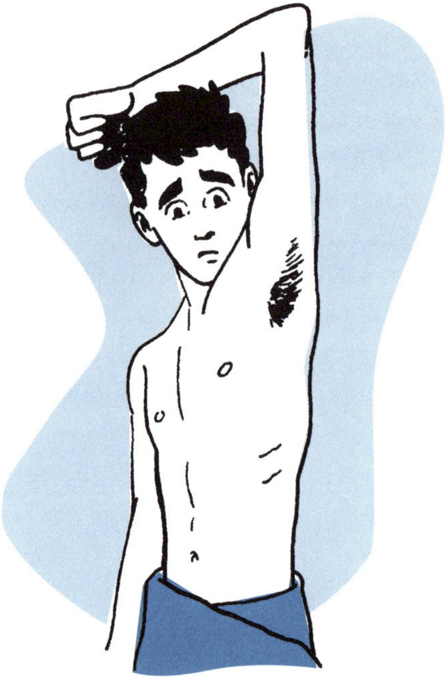

"Another of these changes is the gradual appearance of hair on different parts of your body—under your armpits, in your groins, and on your cheeks and upper lip. No, you haven't got a mustache yet, but it looks as if you might be starting one."

notice, may feel greasy or dry and scaly and uncomfortable; you think everybody is noticing how bad it makes you look.

"Another of these changes is the gradual appearance of hair on different parts of your body–under your armpits, in your groins, and on your cheeks and upper lip. No, you haven't got a mustache yet, but it looks as if you might be starting one. Some of you have even taken a crack at Dad's razor or electric shaver. (Better put it back exactly where he keeps it, if you have. He's probably touchy about such things.)

"Possibly what's bothered you more than anything else is that you've begun to be clumsy as you never used to be when you were smaller and younger. You sometimes stumble over your big feet when you come into a room, especially if there happen to be strangers there and you feel a little bit uncomfortable in front of them. Maybe you knock over a glass of water at the table when you reach for it with those long arms of yours, which is pretty unpleasant if the folks are having company. You never used to be so clumsy and do such awkward things. Why should you suddenly get that way, now that you are older and ought to have *more* control instead of *less*? 'What's the matter with me, anyway?' you think.

"But there certainly can't be any connection between all of these entirely different things, you'd naturally think. Well, if you think that, you are wrong, all wrong. They are all parts of a very strange change that everybody goes through at about the age you fellows are now. They're part of a kind of growth that's entirely different from any growth you've ever gone through, or even known about, before.

"Up to now, you've been growing gradually and steadily, first from small to big, and next from big to bigger, with no change except one of size, as an animal or a tree grows. But now a growth or change has come along that is something of a different kind entirely. For it is a complete alteration that is taking place, one that marks you as being no longer a boy, but a beginning man—though it may take years yet before the change is completed. And the thing that brings all this about is what you've learned in your biology class to call the "glandular system."

"You know of course about the glands that manufacture fluids for doing things in the body that we know about, like the gastric (stomach) and intestinal glands that pour out digestive juices, the skin glands that furnish sweat and oil to keep the skin in good condition, and the tear glands that gave us something to cry with when we were children. We call these glands of external secretion.

"But there are other glands that manufacture something that goes into our bodies and works in a way harder to understand. One of these, the pituitary gland, is a little thing tucked away under the brain that makes our bodies grow big enough, but not too big. Another is the thyroid gland, that makes us alert and keeps us on our toes. If it becomes too active, we get terribly nervous and scary and jittery and big-eyed. But if it's not active enough, we get sluggish and stupid and dull. We call these glands of internal secretion because while we can see the results they cause, we can't see what they produce as we can in the case of the glands of external secretion I've just mentioned.

"There's still a third kind of gland which turns out *both* external *and* internal secretions. One of these, or rather two of these, are the testicles, two plum-sized glands that are contained in the scrotum, a bag that hangs down from the crotch, just behind the penis. We're going to call things by their real names here, you understand, for you lads are big enough now to discuss things like men, and not like kids that have to have baby names for parts of your body and the functions that they perform.

"The internal secretion put out by the testicles is the peculiar fluid that starts off all these changes of growth that you've been noticing in yourselves–the overactivity of the skin glands, the voice changes, the appearance of hair in different parts of the body, and the sudden spurt in height and weight that makes you stumble over your clodhopper feet and fumble things when you miss your aim with your long arms. Stranger still, it brings about differences in the way you think and feel, which is what we call your emotional development.

"This internal secretion put out by the testicles changes you in some mysterious way that no one really understands so that you begin to feel the way a man feels and have some of the thoughts and wishes that a man has and that a younger boy doesn't have. For example, you begin to have courage and backbone and guts that are not expected of a small boy, but are taken for granted in a man. You get more and more interested in girls, where before, as a little fellow, you thought they were just a nuisance to be teased and then pushed aside. You look forward to having more to do with them–first with any girl, later with one particular one.

"After a while you'll find you'd like to be with that girl for most of the time, if she turns out to be just the one you've been looking for. And at last you'll want to marry her and have her for your very own, and have children that are yours and hers.

It will take some years before all this happens, of course; but that's what this mystery juice I'm talking about is already starting to do to you. So you see why I say it's so important.

"Now don't fall for the idea that so many people have, that a deep rumbling voice or lots of hairs on chest and armpits and arms and legs means that a person is more of a he-man than if these were not so pronounced. Many a star athlete has very little hair anywhere except what he wears on top of his head, and a voice that is absolutely tenor.

"Everyone passes through this stage of development that is called adolescence–from two word roots that mean "becoming

"That is why it is so necessary for a boy to follow a doctor's directions after a severe blow is suffered by the testicle, or when he has mumps. Such care usually prevents any permanent damage that might otherwise take place."

adult"–unless for some reason, such as injury or disease, his testicles are unable to do their work. That is why it is so necessary for a boy to follow a doctor's directions after a severe blow is suffered by the testicle, or when he has mumps. Such care usually prevents any permanent damage that might otherwise take place.

"The intentional prevention of the change called adolescence is what takes place when a bull is castrated and thereby changed into a mild-dispositioned ox. The same thing happens when a young stallion is turned into a steady-going horse, or a scrappy, cocky rooster turns into a fat, sluggish capon. In the middle ages this was sometimes done to boys with good singing voices so that they wouldn't change from soprano or alto to tenor or bass. Such persons (called "eunuchs") became fat and flabby and sallow, with wide hips like a woman's. Fortunately, this is never done nowadays, so it need give us no concern here and now.

"So much for the *internal* secretion of the testicles–but what about the "external secretion" that I told you is manufactured by the testicles? This is extremely different in its purpose and actions. It consists of millions of tiny bodies floating in a white substance, which is called "semen," or "spermatic fluid," because it contains the male elements that are called "sperms." One of these will some day leave the body to unite with a female element, the egg or "ovum," that is produced in the ovary of a girl or woman, and will form an "embryo," as the very beginning human being is called.

"Each sperm or male element consists of a tiny head, and a wriggling tail about six times as long, even though altogether a sperm measures not over one five-hundredth of an inch in length! It is hard to believe that the union of two such tiny cells–(for the ovum isn't much larger) so small that they cannot be seen except under a high powered microscope, could ever grow into a seven- or eight-pound baby, or later into a man or woman of 150 or 160 pounds!

"How do these sperms leave the body? There are several way that I'll tell you about later. But telling you this much has taken so long that I'll have to wait till another get-together before going into that. Right now, I'm ready for your questions. Send them along, and let's get started at once, so we'll have plenty of time for everyone. Who'll be the first to ask about something you've been wondering about?"

Chapter 4

QUESTIONS

At the end of the talk, the boys came down to the front of the chapel and crowded around the doctor. The questions came quick and fast; and in order to make the most of what time was left, they had to be answered quickly and to the point. Here they are:

Question. Is it a sign that something is wrong when one testicle hangs down lower than the other?

Answer. No, that's the way it is with everyone. It's usually the left one that hangs lower, though sometimes it's the right. You've probably noticed that both hang down lower after a hot bath, while the scrotum gets tighter and less relaxed after a cold plunge or shower.

Question. What does it mean when there's a hard lump in the scrotum?

Answer. This is usually what is called a hydrocele, and is an accumulation of water. It may have to be drawn off by a surgeon through a hollow needle–not a serious operation at all. If there is a painful lump, however, that is probably an inflammation of the testicle, called orchitis. It should be treated at once, as it may be serious if it is neglected. For anything like this, go to your doctor at once.

Question. But if there's a soft irregular lump that sometimes feels heavy and dragging down, especially after I've been standing or running or doing any heavy exercise, what is that from?

Answer. That is known as a varicocele. It is due to a weakening of the walls of the vein that carries the blood back from the testicle into the body. It's been described as feeling to the examining surgeon like a bunch of angle worms! It can be cured by a simple operation that consists in tying off the weakened vein so that the blood will flow back through other and stronger veins. But it is rarely uncomfortable enough to need any treatment at all.

Question. Is a rupture an indication that a boy isn't perfectly manly?

Answer. Not at all. It simply means that one part of the wall of muscle that keeps the intestine inside the abdomen has a weak spot that has allowed a knuckle or loop of intestine to protrude. Sometimes it can be held back in place by wearing a truss or support that exerts pressure on it, and thus reinforces the weak spot in the muscle wall. It's usually better to have a surgeon sew the sheathes of the muscles together in such a way that this spot is strengthened. It's not a serious operation.

Some of the huskiest athletes develop hernias after strenuous athletic exertion, and have to be operated on. So you see that a rupture, or hernia, is not a sign that a fellow is a weakling.

Question. Does it mean that a boy can never have children if he has only one testicle?

Answer. Not at all. It simply means that there has been a delay in the movement of one of these glands from inside the abdomen (which is where they are normally before birth) down into the scrotum. If it cannot be brought down by medicine or injections, a simple operation will do the trick.

Question. Is it serious if a boy's nipples grow hard and swollen and tender?

Answer. That is a perfectly natural thing to take place during this time of developing into manhood that we've been talking about.

Question. Some of the bigger fellows sometimes pinch or twist a smaller boy's nipples through his clothes so that it hurts. Is there any danger in this?

Answer. Of course there is. Serious damage can occur as a result. Bullying a smaller lad is pretty small potatoes, especially when it can do as much harm as this silly custom does.

Question. What is it when the penis gets hard?–I mean, just what happens?

Answer. Some parts of the penis are spongy, containing very many tiny spaces through which the blood circulates.

"Some of the bigger fellows sometimes pinch or twist a smaller boy's nipples through his clothes so that it hurts. Is there any danger in this?"

Sometimes when a fellow gets to thinking about sex, or even when he is asleep, the return of blood gets cut off, and the organ becomes hard, larger, and rigid, like the fire engine hose under high pressure. When the mechanism for shutting off the returning blood relaxes, it returns to its usual limp, soft condition. This is called an erection.

Question. Some fellows are very sensitive because of the small size of these parts, especially younger boys. I've seen something advertised that is guaranteed to develop them and increase their size. Is there any need for such a thing for fellows like this?

Answer. No, nor for anyone else. The size of the organs of generation has absolutely nothing to do with a person's manliness, or "virility," as it is called. Ads of this sort play on the false idea, based on ignorance, that large parts mean great sex ability. Nothing could be farther from the truth.

These advertisements are nothing but gold bricks, meant to wheedle money out of innocent boobs. They can't accomplish what they promise, of course; and even if they could, it would do no good.

Question. Do they develop faster in some people than in others?

Answer. Yes, just as some boys are slower in developing hair on their chests, and some people get teeth later than other people. For that matter, they never get as large in some men as they do in others; but this doesn't affect their sex life at all.

Question. Doesn't a shot of liquor increase a fellow's ability to be–er–manly?

Answer. Not in the slightest. What it does do is simply to make him think he's more of a man than he actually is! Even a little drink makes a fellow's opinion of himself go up, while it also strengthens his desires. At the same time it blunts the good sense and self-restraint that might otherwise have kept him from doing harm to a girl he's supposed to be reliable enough to be with. And its avoidance might well prevent him from getting a disease, or from becoming the father of an illegitimate child. You can imagine what a tragedy either of these must be!

That's all for today. See you again before too long.

Chapter 5

TWO BIG PROBLEMS

"There, that tough job is over and done with," growled the doctor, as the last of the group of prospective campers stepped off the office scale and started to dress. "You're none of you perfect specimens of manhood, but at least every one of you has passed his physical exam for camp. Now hurry up and dress and get out of here so that I can get some worthwhile work done."

He started to leave the room, when he was halted by a chorus of howls and jeers. He turned round in time to see a flustered Tom stoop down and reclaim a bulldog briar pipe that had clattered to the floor from the pocket of the trousers some thoughtful friend had tied in a hard knot while he was on the scale.

"So what?" countered Tom belligerently. "You've all seen me smoke, even if Doc hasn't. As far as that goes, most of you do, too, though you're not men enough to come out and do it in the open.

"But when you come right down to it, what harm does it do us? Most of our dads and half our mothers smoke, and it hasn't killed them. Why should we wait till we're eighteen, or twenty-one, or whatever it is they tell us to wait till, before we start? Go right ahead and say what you're thinking, though I know you don't approve, Doc."

It was a question they had all asked themselves. They looked expectantly at the doctor, knowing that he would give them the straight of it if they asked for it.

"Sit down and I'll tell you exactly what I think. You've used up half my lunch period, so I may as well waste another few minutes. How do you know I don't approve, Wise Guy? Did I ever let on that I knew that you, or any of the rest of you, were smoking? How do you suppose I could tell?" He caught Jim's hand and held it up so that everyone could see the yellow stains on his index and middle fingers. "Don't ask me why I'm such a keen private eye. It's perfectly simple," and the doctor smiled his exasperating smile.

"Of course you couldn't approve openly, or our folks would all say you were a 'bad influence,'" Tom defended himself. "But honestly, just what *is* wrong with smoking, anyway? I know you're not a smoker, yourself. Suppose you tell us why not, if you can take the time?" The boys squatted in a circle on the examination room floor, the doctor swung one leg over the examining table in what looked like an extremely uncomfortable position, but which he seemed to like, and began.

"In the first place, I don't consider it any of my business whether you smoke or not. I do think it's *your* business, though, to decide whether you're doing the square thing when you smoke behind your parents' backs. I've known lots of men, and a lot of doctors among them, who are convinced that there's no harm in their smoking. But I've never yet known anyone, even if he himself smoked behind the barn when he was ten, who would come out and say he believed smoking is desirable, or even that it's harmless, for a boy of fourteen or fifteen."

"But doesn't it stunt your growth? That's what my grand-dad says he always used to be told. But he's a pretty tough old six-footer, so it didn't seem to interfere with *his* growth," and Jack sat back with a satisfied smile, as if he had spiked at least one argument.

"It's extremely difficult for scientific observers to deliver an impartial verdict on such a very personal question as smoking," the doctor answered thoughtfully. "Doctors are much like other people–they do pretty much what they want to do, and then look around and try to find or make up reasons to justify themselves.

"I can refer you to what the writers honestly intend to be scientific articles, both for and against; but I can honestly say I don't know which are the more truly impartial and to be believed. Some doctors say smoking is bad for some forms of heart disease; others say that's nonsense, and that moderate smoking is calming to the nerves. Some observers are convinced that the undoubted increase in the number of cases of cancer of the lung has a definite relationship to the increase in smoking and especially inhaling of cigarette smoke. I certainly shouldn't dare to venture an opinion, when the authorities disagree."

"But *you* don't smoke; so you must think it's bad," suggested Jim.

"As for myself, I've never seen enough advantages in it to make me feel it was worth my while to begin. For I know that if I did it once, I'd probably never quit. I know a lot of men and women that do try to stop every once in a while, and they are miserable when they're not smoking. It's funny, but you never hear anybody rave over how much he enjoys it while he *is* smoking.

"Some people have to be always doing something with their hands, but I'm not the fidgety kind. Some folks, women especially, but a lot of men and boys, too, are "slaves to fashion." They just have to be doing what they think the majority of people are doing, or they feel out of line and sort of inferior, or ill at ease. I've never felt that anyone cared a hoot whether I smoked or not. Most smokers never count up what the habit costs them. But you know, and I know, that it must cost plenty. I have a lot of ways to spend money that I get more fun out of. All in all, I can't see that the good things outweigh the disadvantages, for me–and for a lot of other folks, as well. But that's *their* business, not mine.

"So now you know what I think about my smoking, and about yours. But don't think I'm going to snitch about Tom's pipe–or about Harry's coffin nails, either," and he deftly twitched a pack of well-known brand from the shirt pocket of the boy who squatted at his feet. "Now hustle, or you'll be late to the basketball game," and he shooed the group into the hall.

As the boys trooped out, Harry called to Bill, "Hurry up, Romeo! Don't keep Anne waiting, or she'll be sitting the game out with your rival. Or maybe you'd rather go moping down Lover's Lane, or necking in the movies." Harry ducked Bill's swinging left, and the others grinned appreciatively, while Jack, the youngest, looked rather disgusted at the whole by-play.

Dropping behind as the others crowded out the door, Jack turned to the doctor with a puzzled air. The doctor waited encouragingly, and the boy began:

"I say, doctor, just what is the fun in what the older fellows are always beating their gums about–petting, or necking, or boodling? Is it the same as what the older people used to call spooning? How can a fellow who's as good an athlete and all-round outdoor man as Bill stand it to stay hanging around with some girl who isn't interested in a single thing a boy enjoys doing? I just don't get it."

"You will before too long, Jack; you will. Do you remember what I told you fellows in school the other day about the changes that take place in your bodies about the age you are now? Well, there are other changes that you're probably just beginning to notice, though as yet you're just a little ashamed to admit it.

"Up until a little while ago, you weren't the least bit interested in girls, and you couldn't understand why the other fellows were such saps as to fall for them, and the sissy stuff that went with it all.

"But now you're beginning to have a change in the way you feel about them, though it makes you mad to have to admit it. Before, all the use you had for girls was to tease them, and be mean to them, and feel how superior you were to them. Now

"How can a fellow who's as good an athlete and all-round outdoor man as Bill stand it to stay hanging around with some girl who isn't interested in a single thing a boy enjoys doing? I just don't get it."

you don't know why it is, but you kinda like to be with them—or maybe to be with one particular certain one of them. The other fellows are beginning to notice it, and they rag you about it. You get back by riding some other boy for doing and feeling the same way you do.

"So far, you just like to be with her and talk with her, though you're ashamed to have anybody notice it. But a little while later on, when more of that change from boy to man that we talked about gets to working in you, you'll want to get close to her, and put your arm around her, and maybe even kiss her. Or maybe it'll be some other girl you feel that way about. It would be very unusual if this change didn't take place in you.

"Now a certain amount of this is, as I say, perfectly all right. But after a while it is likely to go too far and get to the point of wanting to be closer and closer, so that you may suddenly wake up and find that you feel terribly like doing something you know you ought not to do, like touching other parts of her body.

"Some day, when you are a little bit farther along on this road that every boy has to travel, I'll talk with you some more about it. But that's as far as we need to go today, anyway. If you'll only remember to do what you know is right, you can have a whale of a good time with girls. And what's more, you'll be doing the square thing by them and by yourself. Meanwhile, don't be too scornful about the way Bill and some of the other older Joes are acting. You'll be there yourself the first thing you know.

"Now get going and catch up with the rest of the mob. Get into the cheering section and yell your head off for your team. If one particular girl is where she can see you, I'll bet you'll split a lung trying to outdo the others–but you won't admit it. G'bye now," and the door closed behind the doctor, as Jack walked slowly down the street, uncertain as to how much of what had been said was really true.

Chapter 6

GIRLS

Two weeks later the doctor again found himself on the chapel platform before a hundred eager listeners waiting for him to take up where he had left off. He began with no introduction:

"When I saw you before, I told you that the next time we discussed things, I was going to explain to you how the sperms, or male cells, left a boy's body, and what happened to them. But after thinking it over, I have decided that something else ought to come first. I shall, therefore, describe to you how a girl's or woman's body differs from ours, and tell you something of its function in this business of making more people so as to keep up the supply of folks in this world of ours.

"Now I know that many of you fellows have been told all sorts of things that aren't so–sometimes by people that don't know any better, and sometimes by folks that are just plain lying. Nobody likes being played for a sucker, so I am going to give you the straight of it. If I don't make things clear, interrupt and stop me as we go along; or ask anything you want to after I've finished.

"You remember, don't you, that I told you last time about the three different kinds of glands—external secretion, internal secretion, and both kinds at once—and that the testicles belong to the third class, those that have both external and internal secretions. If you have given it any thought at all, you've probably guessed that girls and women must have some glands that are somewhat like these that perform the same duties. In the first place, there would have to be some sort of female cells to unite with the male cells to make new people. And in the second place, there would have to be something to change little girls into big girls, and then into women as they grow older, just as you and I have to be changed from boys into men.

"If you reasoned this way, you'd be what they call a 'logician'—a fellow who uses his head to reason out the causes that bring about certain effects. And you'd be dead right. For there *are* such glands; and they are very much like the testicles in a man or boy. They do produce another magic fluid that can't be seen, but that changes girls and makes them grow up into women, who act so different and look so different from the way we boys and men do. And at the same time, they manufacture female cells that can join with male cells to make the beginnings of new human beings. These glands are called the ovaries.

"If you've ever had a bad stomach ache, bad enough to call the doctor for, you'll probably remember how he poked around all over your poor sore tummy, but especially on the lower right side, to see whether you had appendicitis. Well, near this spot in girls lies the right ovary; and in the same spot on the left side, the left ovary. They are about the same size and shape as the testicles, and they act in girls just about the same way that the testicles do in boys. They never get outside of the body, though, the way the testicles do, but always stay inside the abdomen, just as the testicles did before birth.

"They produce an internal secretion that causes girls to change into women. About every four weeks they produce an egg (ovum in Latin). Let's see what happens to this ovum–where it goes, and what organ in the body receives it, and what becomes of it.

"Lying right between the two ovaries there's a hollow organ about the size and shape of a small pear, called the womb, or uterus. A tiny tube runs from this to each ovary; and along one of these tubes a tiny egg travels from the ovary to the uterus each month. Each is about 1/125 of an inch across. That is quite a little larger than the sperms I told you about last time.

"If a male cell meets this egg somewhere in its course along the tube from the ovary to the uterus and unites with it, we say that it has become fertilized; and an embryo is what is formed. That's the way life began for every one of us here, and for every other human being that ever was born. Pretty big jump from a speck so small you can't see it without a microscope, to a big lug like one of you, wasn't it? Then this tiny fertilized seed has to travel to the uterus, where it will be allowed to grow for the next nine months.

"Now what do you suppose the womb does so that it can take care of such an egg, if it gets fertilized? For it has to get ready for that job every month, even if it never receives a fertilized egg. It does this by thickening its lining so as to provide a warm cozy nest where the fertilized egg, or embryo, can be fed and kept warm for nine months until it is ready to leave the uterus and come out into the world as a live baby.

"But if it doesn't get fertilized–and of course it is only very rarely that it does–then it has to be thrown out of the body. And along with it at the same time go shreds of this thickened lining, together with a certain amount of blood. But this doesn't happen in a minute or a few minutes–it may take as long as a week, or as little time as three days. As it happens every month, more or less, it is called the monthly flow, or menstrual period (from the Latin word for month).

"While this is perfectly normal, it is a time of discomfort for some girls, and they are advised not to do any very hard exercise nor to bathe in very cold water at these times. So if a girl tells you that she can't go on a hike or play some active game or go swimming when she's made a date to do so, it's good sense to know there's probably a sound reason. Don't be dumb and ask too many questions.

"That reminds me that it doesn't hurt any boy to remember once in a while that no matter how much of a tomboy a girl may be, she can't be expected to be quite so rugged and tough as a boy. Instead of teasing her and trying to make her feel inferior, a fellow shows himself a much better sport if he gives her a break and a helping hand once in a while. It's the guy that's really tough and rugged and strong that doesn't have to keep throwing his weight around to show people how good he is.

"Now come on down here in front, any of you who want to stick me with questions. I'll do my best to answer 'em as fast as you can put 'em across."

Chapter 7

MORE QUESTIONS

The boys were a little slow about opening up on this rather unfamiliar topic. But they thawed quickly and showed interest when one of the younger teachers, a fellow quite popular with the boys and especially with the football squad, stepped up and asked a question.

Question. Haven't you seen ads in drug stores and magazines telling girls they don't have to take care during their periods, but can dance and swim and hike just the same as at other times? Yet you seem to tell us just the opposite. Which is right–you, or the ads?

Answer. Both of us. You'll remember I said *some* girls have considerable discomfort; that they shouldn't indulge in *hard* exercise, or bathe in *very cold* water. The ads are talking about girls *in general*; but a boy doesn't know whether the girl in question is, or is not, one of these. So I say it's better to play safe and not be either nosey or persistent if a girl seems to want to skip a date.

Question. Why is it, if as you say it's so terrible for a girl to let a boy go too far, that so many of them try to lead a fellow along and tease him into trying to do what you say he ought not to do?

Answer. That's a question with a whole lot of possible answers. Some girls are unhappy at home and would be glad to spite their parents by doing things they know they would feel bad to have their daughter do. Some like to show their power over boys and brag of their "conquests" to the other girls. And some girls don't realize how much easier it is for a boy to get excited than it is for them, and how much harder it is for a boy to stop once he's started, though sometimes it's the other way around.

Question. Is that why so many girls dress so as to show off the shape of their breasts, or other parts of their body that boys would think they ought to keep covered, if they were girls of the right sort–and yet we know that a lot of those who do this are really the nicest sort of girls?

Answer. That's another tricky question that it would take us much too long to try to answer completely here. Some do it because they think it's the smart thing to imitate the movie stars. More do it, I imagine, because it's the fashion, and some folks would pass out if they didn't follow the fashions. Some do it, as I said just now, to tease boys along and see what effect it may have on the boys that take them out when they go to places where it's easy to forget what's right and what's wrong. And there are still other girls who are honestly and truly too innocent, or too ignorant, to know how such things impress fellows, and what they naturally think about the morals of the girls who dress that way. Even their mothers may not know how boys think and feel about such things; while many fathers have forgotten about how they felt when they were boys.

Question. Is there any harm in kissing a girl good night, or holding hands in the dark in the moving pictures, especially when they're having pretty warm close-ups?

Answer. Well, I'd say that depends pretty much on how you feel about the girl you're with when you're doing it. If it makes you want to keep on and on and to go much farther than you know you ought to, or if you find it hard to stop–or if that's the main thing you think about when you're planning to go out somewhere with her–then I think it's smart to watch your step!

Question. Why do so many older girls keep telephoning you, and want you to take them to the movies, or buy them candy and cokes, or spend a lot of money on them when you haven't got a big allowance? Why can't they leave a fellow alone?

Answer. Well, of course there are some girls who feel that they can't get dates any other way. And of course there *are* fellows who are grafters and like to be invited to go places, especially if they are clever enough to make the girls pay for them! Some girls are willing to pay for boys who have no more pride than to be tame cats that way. This doesn't apply to the sensible plan of "going Dutch," which is perfectly all right, of course. And there are some girls who are uncomfortable when they

"Why do so many older girls keep telephoning you, and want you to take them to the movies, or buy them candy and cokes, or spend a lot of money on them when you haven't got a big allowance? Why can't they leave a fellow alone?"

are with older boys or men, and feel much more at ease with boys of your age.

Question. Some people say you can tell by looking at a girl's face in some way when she is menstruating. Is that true?

Answer. No–no more than it is true, as some people think, that you can tell by a boy's face whether or not he masturbates. Both are silly ideas that have absolutely no truth in them.

Question. I've been told that those long, drawn-out kisses, longer even than those you see in the movies, can cause a girl to have a baby. Is that true?

Answer. No, except that such kisses may excite the boy and the girl and lead them to do other things that may end up with the girl's having a baby! That's why that sort of kissing, and the other things that are just as exciting, had better be put off until after folks are married, when having a baby is what most people want. Having a baby before marriage is something that can and frequently does ruin a girl's chances for happiness for the rest of her life. And it can stop a boy's chances for any more education and future advancement if, as sometimes happens, he is forced into marrying her.

Question. What is an abortion? And wouldn't that save them both from the sort of trouble you speak of?

Answer. Unfortunately, no. In the first place, an abortion, which means destroying the life of the fetus, or embryo, or infant before it comes out of the mother's womb and into the world, is a crime for which there is serious punishment. Then, too, it is so dangerous that it may ruin a girl's health, make her sterile (so that she can't ever have a baby) or even kill her outright. So you see that the cure is worse than the disease!

"After all, fellows," as the doctor ended his talk and started for the door, "there's a lot of satisfaction in being decent, and a good sport, and having the feelings toward girls and women we all know the right sort of boys and men have. We know they're not as strong as we are and so are entitled to our protection; and it just isn't cricket to harm them or make trouble for them. And that's what immorality does–it degrades.

"There are lots of ways of having good times with girls. Let's not choose the wrong ones," and the doctor slipped out the door and got into his car.

Chapter 8

DOCTOR, CAN YOU TELL ME?

Just as the doctor was about to slam the car door, one of the boys who had crowded around, and who had seemed most interested but had asked no questions, ran up to the car door and asked:

"Can you give me a lift, Doctor?"

"Sure, jump in." The doctor slammed the door, and they rode for a minute or two without speaking. Then the boy broke the silence:

"Doctor, there's something that's been bothering me a lot lately. I think I must be terribly vicious, or rotten, or something. For whenever I see some of these pictures in magazines on newsstands of women without much on in the way of clothes, or when I hear the other guys talking about the dames they've done things with, my mind gets to working, and I think all sorts of smutty things.

"I know I oughtn't to do this. But somehow I can't seem to help it. I know I ought to have a strong enough will to make myself think right thoughts, not wrong ones. But somehow or other, the more I try to stop having these thoughts, the more I keep on, and the worse it gets. Why am I so different from other guys who are clean-minded? Why can't I make my mind stay as clean as theirs?"

They rode in silence for two or three minutes. Then the doctor remarked quietly:

"You're not one bit different from most of the rest of us, Don. It's perfectly natural and normal for you to begin to have mental images starting up, after looking at these suggestive pictures or hearing smutty talk. There would probably be something to worry about if you didn't.

"It's this almost universal male tendency to have sexual thoughts that makes writers and editors of books and magazines play up the sexy side of life and exaggerate it in pictures and type. Folks want to sell what they make, and writers and publishers are no different from other people in this respect.

"But there's something a lot worse than this. You've probably heard that there's a several-million-dollar business based on the publication and sale of what is known as 'pornographic material.' What we used to call 'French post cards' have been blown up into a vast, disreputable, and criminal industry whose purpose is to make lots of money by debauching young people. The government is doing its best to run this to earth and stamp it out. But it crops up again and again."

"Yeah, I know," answered Don. "Some of the fellows in school pass these filthy pictures around. I've even known them to show them to nice girls, though they're more likely to show them to girls they know aren't too particular. They get me to thinking these crummy thoughts, too, though I know I oughtn't to."

"Don," said the doctor earnestly, "the next time anything of this sort turns up, and you get to thinking these thoughts, I'd like you to do your best to make yourself remember two things. The first is that while you can't do one single thing to keep the birds from flying in the sky over your head, you certainly don't have to let them light there, mess up your hair, and even build their nests there!

"You can't stop them from flying over your head. The upper air is free, and no matter what silly things you might do to try to stop them, you couldn't. So you let them fly, and pay no attention to them.

"The other thing I'd like you to remember is that there is no such thing as a 'psychological negative.' Sounds very technical, doesn't it? But in reality it's very simple. Let me give you an example of what it means.

"Suppose I were to say to you, 'Now don't think about the end of your nose. Whatever else you do, *don't think about the end of your nose*! Now, remember what I say, Don, *you must not think about the end of your nose*!!!'

"You'd probably tell me, if you were not too polite, 'Well, if you'll only stop telling me not to think about it, I won't. But as long as you keep telling me *not* to think about it, and as long as I keep trying *not* to think about it, I simply can't help thinking about it.'

"That's what is meant by the law, 'There is no such thing as a psychological negative.' You cannot 'not think' about something. All you can do is to think about something else. So don't be worried if these smutty thoughts keep flying over your head. Don't waste a minute trying to 'not think' about them. Just think about something else.

"Don't let yourself think for one moment that you have a dirty mind, or that there must be something wrong about you because you sometimes 'think unclean thoughts.' I have them, too, Don, and so does every other normal boy or man, though not everyone will admit it."

"One thing more," the doctor emphasized firmly. "Don't let yourself think for one moment that you have a dirty mind, or that there must be something wrong about you because you sometimes 'think unclean thoughts.' I have them, too, Don, and so does every other normal boy or man, though not everyone will admit it. You're perfectly normal in this respect, just like most of the rest of us. So quit 'low rating' yourself.

"Just one thing more. Whenever you happen to see any boy passing these dirty pictures around, go at once to your teacher or principal, your pastor or your doctor, or come to me if you want to, and tell what you have seen. No, that's not 'tale-bearing,' or 'snitching,' or 'tattling.' It's just being a good citizen and helping the government get this mental garbage removed to where it can't contaminate decent people."

"But what ought a guy to do when someone begins to tell smutty stories? I can't seem to bring myself to tell them they shouldn't. That looks too 'goody goody,' or like the 'holier than thou' attitude I've read about."

"Neither can I," replied the doctor. "But what you can do, and I can too, is to show pretty plainly, without saying one word, that you don't think that sort of crummy talk is either funny or clever. Don't think for a moment that your example doesn't count. You can be one of the fellows who set a standard of decency in your school. I'd hate to be known, as I've known folks to be, as a guy with a whole string of dirty jokes. That's the sort of a rep I don't want any part of."

They rode on without further discussion until the doctor drew up in front of his office, when Don said:

"Before you go in, Doctor, there's one thing more I'd like to ask you about. It's this business of cheating in school. Almost everyone seems to be doing it, so maybe it's not so terrible. But it gets a guy into a lot of trouble if the teacher finds it out. And besides, I know, way down deep inside me, that it is *not* all right.

"I'm still scared it will come out somehow that I cheated on our last final exam. I know you won't blab, so I can tell you the truth about it. I'm sure I'm no worse than most of the rest of the class. But I can't help feeling that I'm doing wrong when I get help from someone else. What ought I to do about it?" And he looked relieved, now that he had made a clean breast of what it was that had been bothering him.

The doctor sat thinking, while the motor idled. Then he turned off the ignition and began, thoughtfully:

"You've opened up a big problem. The school authorities have never solved it, and I'm sure you and I can't find the answer either. But it *is* something you have to settle for yourself. And maybe I can help you think it through.

"If I were you, I'd figure out a line of conduct for myself. That was what I did when I was your age and was worried over what seemed to me to be the almost universal custom among my classmates of looking at the other guy's paper, or passing notes from one to the other when the teacher wasn't looking.

"I made up my mind to do what I knew was the honest thing and not get mixed up with something I knew was wrong, even though it did seem to be done pretty constantly. Nobody ever seemed to feel that I thought I was 'holier than thou.' But the others knew I didn't either ask or give help, so I wasn't bothered. It sure made school a lot pleasanter to have a good conscience, instead of always having a guilty conscience and wondering when things would come to the surface and trouble would start for everyone.

"It will help you over a lot of uncomfortable times, Don, if you'll try to bear this one thing in mind. Like everyone else, and especially like everyone around your age, you are inclined to be in a good deal of doubt about yourself. Even folks that appear to others to be 'stuck on themselves' aren't as a rule too certain of themselves. So they try extra hard to make everyone else think they are tops. They wouldn't do that if they felt certain that they were. It's that old 'inferiority reaction' or 'inferiority complex' that folks talk so much about."

"That's quite a new idea to me," replied Don, thoughtfully. "But I believe you're right. That *is* what's the matter with me. But what can a guy do to get over that feeling?"

"I don't suppose we ever get over it completely," answered the doctor. "And maybe it's just as well that we don't. But if you will try to stop analyzing yourself and thinking about your feelings all the time and get out instead with other people and take an active part in what is going on, you can keep this inferiority feeling from getting you down.

"So glad you felt like talking these things over with me. You know I'm your friend, and I'm never too busy to chat with you. Drop around any time you get up against something that bothers you."

Both got out, and they parted at the doctor's door.

“Thanks a million, Doctor. You’ve sure answered my questions, and you’ve made me feel a lot better.” And the lad heaved a deep breath as if he’d had a load lifted from his chest.

“Come back with more questions any time you feel like it. I may not have all the answers, but I’ll do the best I can.” The doctor thrust his key into the door latch while Don walked slowly down the street.

Chapter 9

THE RACE MUST GO ON

The next time the doctor came to school, he felt like quite an old hand; and the boys, knowing what to expect in the way of a discussion, were all ready to go. They were not disappointed. The doctor came directly to the point:

"I promised you the first day I talked with you that I'd tell you how the male elements, or sperms, leave the body of the boy or man. Now that seems a simple enough thing to do, but it really packs quite a punch, for it opens up almost everything that worries a boy who hasn't had these things explained to him fully and clearly. That's exactly what I'm going to do for you fellows today. If there's anything I've skipped over or haven't explained clearly and you haven't nerve enough to ask me about it, it's your funeral, not mine. All I can do is promise to tell you everything you want to know. So here's the low-down.

"The first way that the semen, the fluid containing the male elements, leaves the body is by means of what are properly called 'nocturnal emissions,' because they take place at night, during sleep. Boys usually call them 'wet dreams.' There are so many mistaken ideas about these and what causes them, and these ideas worry boys so, that I want you to know just what they are and what they mean.

"You remember I told you that the testicles make these sperms and store them in the body, floating about in a thick whitish fluid called semen. Whenever the storage tanks get too full, they empty themselves. Sometimes they do this at night, when a boy is dreaming about sex matters. Sometimes they do it without any sign at all except that the night clothing or bed clothes may be wet or discolored. This may happen several nights in succession, or as seldom as several weeks apart, or in some boys hardly ever.

"Do these do any harm? No indeed–unless a boy doesn't understand how perfectly harmless they are, and worries over them, especially if he thinks that they are his fault. If he is told that they come because of so-called 'impure thoughts' he may have had, he should not believe it, for it's not so. Every normal boy has such thoughts at times, and they do no harm as long as he doesn't brood over them and keep thinking about them. And whether he does or not they have absolutely nothing to do with nocturnal emissions, which are just as natural and normal for a boy to have as menstruation is for a girl. They are a helpful safety valve. Nothing he can do can prevent them, fortunately, for that might be like tying down the safety valve on an engine.

"But they can do a great deal of harm if a fellow is foolish enough to listen to ignorant or crooked advisers, or if he hap-

"Whenever the storage tanks get too full, they empty themselves. Sometimes they do this at night, when a boy is dreaming about sex matters. Sometimes they do it without any sign at all except that the night clothing or bed clothes may be wet or discolored."

pens to see and believe some of the advertisements that used to be commonly seen in public rest rooms. It is surprising how many a Joe you'd think would have more sense, falls for this stuff and proves to be a soft touch for some advertising quack who tells him that these are 'draining away his manhood'– whatever that may mean!

"Is there anything at all to that kind of mullarky? Absolutely none at all–take my word for it. So if any of you fellows have been worrying that you were being harmed by these dreams, or that you must be dirty minded or you wouldn't have them and the thoughts that sometimes go along with them after you wake up, stop worrying.

"Above all, don't let anybody take you for a ride and get money out of you on the false claim that he can 'cure' you by exercises or medicine. You can't cure someone who's well already! And if that's all that's the matter with you, you sure are very well indeed!

"Now there is another way in which the semen, or seminal fluid, can leave the body, and sometimes does. This is from something that I suppose every normal boy that ever lived in this world has done at some time or other. And that is rubbing or handling his penis until it causes a pleasant sensation that is usually followed by the forcible ejection of some whitish fluid, which of course is the semen we've been talking about. And this, which has been given the name of masturbation, is something about which there's been more misinformation and pure bunk than any other thing I can think of at the moment.

It's perfectly natural that every boy at some time or other should discover a pleasant sensation could be had by doing just this very thing. He may find it out by himself by accident; he may be told and shown about it by other fellows of the wrong sort who enjoy getting younger boys into trouble, and exerting power over them through fear of exposure.

Any boy knows by instinct that this is something he ought not to do; but it is pleasant, and so he keeps on doing it, but tries to keep it a dead secret. Sooner or later someone finds out about it, and then the trouble starts!

"If it happens to be the boy's father or mother who makes the 'awful' discovery, and they have the usual mistaken ideas about its seriousness, they'll probably be terribly worried and think that he's contracted a habit that is going to harm him for life. They may accuse him as though it were some terrible thing he is guilty of. Or maybe they'll go in deep shame and embarrassment to their doctor and confess that their son is guilty of such an awful thing that they can hardly force themselves to mention it even in the strictest confidence.

"It's surprising how difficult it often is for a doctor to convince these good people that what their son has been doing is not some dreadfully shameful act, but simply what probably every boy has done. The very fact that in all probability the father himself did it when he was a boy, and of course got over the habit as every normal person does, makes him just that much more indignant and frightened and critical, all the same time, about his own boy.

"The doctor will be doing the whole family–father, mother, and son–the greatest service if he can convince them of the truth of what I've just been telling you. That is that it's nothing at all to worry over, and that the sooner they and the boy realize this reassuring fact–and it *is* a fact I can assert without fear of contradiction–the sooner he'll master the habit and leave it behind him, just as he leaves all his other kid habits behind him.

"In fact, I've found that one of the most helpful things I can do is to tell them on my word of honor that it's not much more serious than thumb sucking! Of course no one would want a boy to go on sucking his thumb till he grew to be a man. But we certainly don't feel that it's a family disgrace that a boy used to suck his thumb. He got over the one childhood habit–and he'll get over this other one, if he is not badgered and heckled and everlastingly scared into continually thinking about it, and the awful results he's been told will follow it. That's the surest way in the world to make him continue the habit.

"We come now to the third and most important way the male elements can leave the man's body. This is by intercourse. The purpose of this, as you can see from what we've been talking about, is for a sperm to unite with an ovum to form an embryo that will eventually grow into another man or woman.

"Now there are two entirely different ways in which this can take place. The one way is natural, normal, and right. The other way is wrong, and always brings trouble of some sort or other as a result.

"The first way is marriage. Here a man and a woman choose each other over everybody else in the whole world, just as your own father and mother did, and promise to live together and make a home for themselves and the children they may bring into the world. This is the natural way, the purpose for which sex was provided.

"But there is another way, that is called by the long name, 'promiscuity,' or better, 'immorality.' Here, two people, without either love or respect for each other and without any wish to bring children into the world, have intercourse. This way is unlawful, dangerous, and terribly selfish.

"It is unlawful because it is forbidden by God's law and by the teachings of all religions. It is dangerous, because it frequently causes serious disease. And it is selfish, because in spite of precautions and so-called preventives, it so often brings into the world an innocent baby who has to go through life with the undeserved shame of being known as illegitimate, or a bastard.

"I've given you a long enough lecture for today. No, you needn't applaud. I'll take your word for it that you weren't bored!"

The doctor smiled as the boys shuffled their feet and started for the doors.

Chapter 10

STILL MORE QUESTIONS

In spite of prof's suggestion that the doctor do as the boys wanted him to do and run over into the next period, he shook his head, saying simply:

"You fellows have had enough of my talking for one day. If any of you can take any more, come on down here in front and I'll answer anything that you ask me. Then we can get on down to the lunchroom before everything is gone."

Most of the boys crowded out through the doors; but several of the older boys came down to the front and milled about as one of their group addressed the doctor:

Question. You haven't told us how the sperms get from where they're made, in the testicles, to outside of the body. Just how do they get out?

Answer. Well, as you say, they're formed in the testicles. A tube with muscular walls, called the vas deferens, runs from each testicle to one of the seminal vesicles. These are reservoirs or storage vats for the semen that the vas deferens sends along to them. When these become full, they empty themselves through another long stretch of the vas deferens into a tube called the urethra.

Question. The urethra? Isn't that the tube that runs through the penis and carries off the urine? Why doesn't that get mixed with the sperms in the semen?

Answer. Because there's a little valve on the bladder that closes whenever the semen is being expelled, so that no urine can leave the bladder until the semen has gone through.

Question. Isn't a boy likely to lose his manhood if he doesn't use these parts of the body you've been telling us about? I've always heard that if you tied up a leg or put an arm in a splint for too long a time, the muscles would wither and become weak and useless because they weren't used. Why wouldn't this happen if a person never had intercourse so as to exercise these organs?

Answer. Because the different systems, male and female, are being "used" actively all the time, in the ways I've been telling you about. The boy's make sperms and "testosterone," the male juice or "hormone." The girl's make ova (eggs) and "estrogen," the female hormone. There's no danger of their withering away from disuse, as a muscle would. A boy who doesn't have intercourse is storing up his manhood, just as a person stores up money in the bank, instead of wasting it.

Question. But I've read that if a boy or girl gets all worked up and excited by petting or reading hot stories or seeing sexy pictures or watching a strip tease at a show and doesn't have intercourse to relieve himself, he gets terribly "frustrated"–whatever that means! Isn't that true? If it isn't so, then some pretty well-known authors are lying, for they write as if that was something everyone admitted.

Answer. Don't fall for everything you see in print. Lots of folks make statements it would be hard for them to prove. It may "frustrate" me (make me feel baffled and unhappy, that is) if I see another doctor driving a Lincoln or a Cadillac, or living in a mansion on millionaire's row, or making some wonderful scientific discovery. But that doesn't excuse me if I steal a car or rob a bank so as to have what I want so badly. Instead, I'll land in the jailhouse.

But if my desire to have these things makes me work harder to get them than I otherwise would, then instead of being made unhappy by not having them, I may be spurred on to work harder so that I can earn them for myself. In the very same way, the fact that a boy or girl doesn't snatch at the questionable pleasure of intercourse (and believe me, many a boy and girl who've grabbed at it in this hasty, wrong way have found it a long way from pleasurable) may make them willing to work and wait and earn the real pleasure of marriage.

Question. What about one of the older fellows in the senior class who's always sounding off about the girls he's "made" who've never fallen for anyone before?

Answer. He tries to make other fellows think he's a hot shot. That shows that he feels shaky about himself and has to build himself up in that cheap way–the only way he can beat the decent fellows. The rest of you know him for the louse he is.

Question. What is circumcision?

Answer. It's cutting off a small layer or fold of skin that covers the glans, or end of the penis. It's a religious rite for some people, and a means of insuring cleanliness for some others.

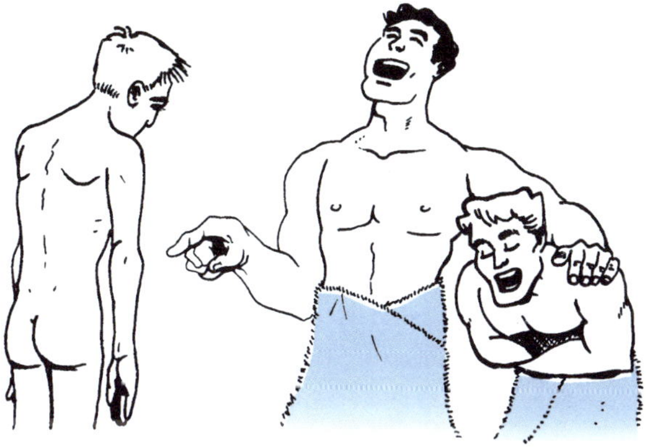

"We used to josh one boy in our gym class who had such a long foreskin he was ashamed to take a shower where the other fellows could see him. Why was he so different from the rest of us?"

Question. We used to josh one boy in our gym class who had such a long foreskin he was ashamed to take a shower where the other fellows could see him. Why was he so different from the rest of us?

Answer. That small difference meant nothing at all. But fellows are pretty cruel, or at least mighty thoughtless, the way they make fun of anyone who's the least bit different from the average. If such a foreskin is tight, as well as long, it might be wise for him to be circumcised so that he could keep himself clean more easily. But that is something for his doctor to advise him about.

Question. If, as you say, it isn't necessary to use these parts so as to develop them, why would anyone buy something I saw advertised that was guaranteed to increase their size?

Answer. It isn't necessary. As I told you before, the size of these parts has nothing whatever to do with a fellow's manliness or "virility," as it's sometimes called.

Question. What I can't understand is what makes older fellows, and sometimes even men that you'd think were decent people, try to get boys to let them do things to them that they know they ought not to.

Answer. If anybody of that sort ever gets to fooling around with you, or with any boys you know, don't be sucker enough to fall for it or let them get away with it. Don't hesitate for one minute to tell someone in authority exactly what has happened, or what you have seen or know. No matter how fine a man he seems to be, or how respected he is in the community, any man who tries to get you to undress, or to let him play with you ought to be shown up for what he is. If it happens around school, go to Prof. Or if it's some boys' club worker as sometimes happens, go to your minister or your Sunday School teacher or superintendent. Or tell your father, or come to me, or go to any older man you have confidence in, and spill it all. You'll be protecting other younger boys, as well as yourself, to say nothing of putting such a crumb where he will be protected from himself. For the law takes a very dim view of that sort of monkey business.

Question. But why would anyone want to do anything like that?

Answer. It would take too long to tell you why some men get their satisfaction out of ruining young boys, and getting them started doing the same sort of thing with other youngsters. They are mentally "off," of course; and they really ought to be taken away for treatment and kept where they can't do any more harm. But until the world wakes up to the fact that such people are dangerous and keeps them separated from the rest of us, you fellows must help locate them.

Question. But won't they say you're a tattletale, or a sissy, or a poor sport, or a spy, if you do that?

Answer. Do you call a plainclothesman, or an F.B.I. agent, or an underground revolutionist in a country behind the Iron Curtain a poor sport? That sort of thing takes a lot more guts than almost anything I know of; and men get pretty important citations and decorations for going beyond the call of duty that way. The only way you can fight that kind of dirty undercover corruption that Tom speaks of, is with the counter-fire of good common sense and fine citizenship.

If you saw a crook snatching a purse, or a second story man entering the house of one of your friends, you'd send in an alarm for the police, wouldn't you? Sure, you would. So don't fall for any such false reasoning from a man or a crowd who are doing more harm, much more, to young boys who can't speak up for themselves, than anybody who lifts a purse or burglarizes a house. They're the ones who are the poorest sort of poor sports. They know that the only way they can be stopped and exposed is by the good sportsmanship of anybody who finds out what they are up to.

Chapter 11

TOM, JIM AND BILL

The doctor's doorbell rang a few days later. He went to the door and let in two boys, Tom and Jim, who were evidently very much disturbed about something. Brought into the consulting room after the last patient had left, they started to speak, stopped, then tried again. Finally Tom blurted out:

"Doctor, is there anything we can do that will keep us from going crazy?"

The doctor guessed what had led to this question, for he had heard it asked several times before. It took a little cross questioning, however, before the boys would admit what had happened. The truth was that Tom's mother had suspected that he was handling his genital organs, and had told him in horrified tones that "the insane asylums are just full of people who have gone crazy because of such self-pollution." What made it worse was that she really believed it, and she was so certain about it and so upset, that the boys believed it too. Of course, Tom at once told Jim.

Both the boys had stayed awake the greater part of that night, and the next, too, and had brooded over the matter pretty steadily ever since. Then they heard the doctor talk in school, but hadn't gotten up courage to ask him about the matter. At last they couldn't stand it any longer, so they came to him in terror to find out if there was anything they could do to save them from this terrible end. They just couldn't believe what he had told them that day.

The answer he was able to give them was prompt, direct and reassuring. He explained that while the habit they had been indulging in was anything but a desirable one, and had once been considered even by doctors to be a very dangerous one, they had nothing to fear. He told them that it is now known to be a scientific fact that, while it is something to be discontinued, it is nothing to worry about, unless they were to carry it on into their later adult years. And he was sure that they had sense enough not to do that.

He told them, as he had told the fellows at school, that it was kid stuff, like thumb sucking, that most sensible fellows succeeded in stopping it when they realized what it was. To be sure, some of the patients in mental hospitals do indulge in the habit. But if they do, it's because they are already mentally unbalanced. They certainly never got that way as a result of masturbating. The belief that that was the cause of their mental condition is all poppycock.

The boys were plainly greatly relieved at what the doctor told them. But there was evidently something more that they hadn't quite gotten up their courage to mention. The doctor realized this; and after waiting for them to go on, he encouraged them:

"Come on, come on, get it off your chests. Come clean with whatever it is that's still eating on you. Let's get it all over with, now that we've gone so far."

After looking at each other to see which should speak first, Jim finally broke down and admitted what was still disturbing them:

"I guess I believe you when you say that most fellows get over this all right. But you see, it's a little different in our case. We've both got 'lost manhood' as a result of what we've been doing for so long. And we haven't got enough money to pay the doctor to cure us, even if it wasn't too late to do anything for us."

"What doctor are you talking about?"

"Why, the one whose address was printed on the poster we saw on the wall of a men's rest room. It explained all about our trouble. It said that 'wet dreams' were a sure sign of 'lost manhood'; and it said for anyone who suffered from these 'night pollutions' to go to his office for treatment. If a fellow wasn't too far gone and could still be cured, he'd try to do what he could for him. Do you suppose there's any hope that he could cure us?"

"That crook is no doctor. He's just a quack, getting blood money from boys and men like yourselves who don't know that reputable physicians never advertise. As I told you the other day, the 'self abuse' and 'secret vice' and 'self pollution' the ad tells about are all silly, old-fashioned names that were used when people thought this bad habit caused all sorts of dreadful things.

"For even if a fellow should slip and give way to it, with some time he'll overcome it.

"I believe you've stopped the habit. So forget all about it. And forget too all the terrible effects you've been reading and hearing about; for I can assure you, you'll never suffer from any of them.

"I wish all the boys and men who are terrified by this sort of dirty advertising had the good sense to talk to someone who knows the score. That would break up this racket. Good night." The doctor led the relieved boys to the door.

As he opened it to let them out, and they started down the front steps toward the street, they saw a boy looking up at them from the foot of the steps. He was somewhat older than Tom or Jim; and the light from the front door showed his pale face and greatly worried expression.

"Sorry, Bill, we waited for you at the corner, but it's too late now," exclaimed Tom, plainly very much disappointed.

"Not a bit of it. Come on in," and the doctor herded them into the dark hall and back to the inner office, switching on his desk light so that it shone on his own face, instead of on theirs, which were thus left in shadow. This made it easier for them to explain the situation. Tom began at once:

"Bill was going to meet us, but he didn't make it. You see, he's got a bad disease, and he's sure it's one that it will take years to cure, if it can be cured at all, which he doubts. How can he go about finding out?"

"What makes him so sure?"

"Well, he's been running around with some of the older men, 'cause he thinks he's too old to be going with us. At least he did think so until last week, when they all went to a beer joint that Bill knew had a bad rep, and hung around with some girls he knew weren't the right sort. After they had bought some drinks, one of them let him spend the night with her in a rooming house near by; and today he's sure he's got a bad disease as a result of what he did."

During all this time, Bill had sat silent, his face in the shadow. The doctor got to his feet, slipped his arm casually about his shoulders, and remarked in a matter of fact tone as he walked toward the door:

"Let's come into the examining room, Bill, and see for sure," and the doctor and Bill disappeared through the open door which closed behind them, leaving Tom and Jim nervously waiting for the bad news they were sure would come out of the room.

It took but a few minutes questioning and a brief but careful examination for the doctor to discover that Bill's imagination, reinforced by a bad conscience, had run away with him and resulted in his making a serious false diagnosis of his condition by exaggerating a few imaginary symptoms. Opening the door of the examining room, he led Bill back to where his friends were anxiously waiting for him. Leaning back in his big leather chair, he told them what he'd discovered.

A blister that had come on Bill's lip after kissing the girl, and that he thought was a syphilitic primary sore or chancre, had proved to be nothing more serious than a cold sore. And the rash on his face was simply an aggravation of a long-standing acne, such as had brought Jack to the doctor at the beginning of our story.

"Bill's in better luck than he has any right to expect," announced the doctor. "There are two very serious diseases, and one other that's not so serious but is terribly painful and annoying, that are frequently caught as the result of the monkey business that Bill engaged in that night last week.

"I'm not going to burden you with an account of all the symptoms, for that would take us half the night. If you care to learn what they are, I'll give you a little Government pamphlet that explains all about them. Next time–if there *is* a next time, for I sure hope and believe that Bill has brains enough to take this as a danger sign and lay off any future playing with dynamite–he might not be quite so lucky."

"But the older men I went there with told me that there were certain sure-fire precautions you could take that would protect you one hundred percent against these diseases. What's more, they said that the same precautions would make it sure that a baby wouldn't come from what you were doing."

"Well, Bill, when they told you that hundred percent yarn, they were getting pretty careless about their figures. There *are* certain precautions that a man can take, and they sometimes work. But they are a long way from perfect, or sure-fire, or one hundred percent effective."

"As far as that goes, even such an apparently simple thing as kissing a girl who has one of these diseases and who doesn't show it–and these diseases are of very common occurrence among both men and women who do the things your pals were doing, and succeeded in getting you to do–can give you either of the two most serious ones. There is only one one hundred percent way to protect yourself–and that is to steer clear of that sort of folks entirely."

Bill let out a long breath that showed his relief and sank back in his chair. But Tom, who had followed all this with the closest attention, plainly had something that was worrying him. The doctor noticed his hesitating manner, and turned toward him, with the air of one who was determined to get it all over with, if it took all night:

"You're next, Tom, so don't lose your turn."

Thus directly appealed to, Tom resolutely took his courage in both hands, and blurted out:

"What's this graveyard stuff that's been going around about one of the girls being taken out of school because she's going to have a baby?"

"Hasn't she been running with a fast crowd–a crowd that you'd hate to see your sister going with?"

"Well, yes, perhaps, though I know my sister would give her favorite compact if they'd take her in. They come from some of the best families in town."

"But that doesn't make them the best boys and girls in town by a long shot. You know that, Jim, and so does everyone else in school. Now if you want to know what's happened, I'll tell you. If you remember what we said about how sperms leave a boy's body, you'll recall that one of the ways was what they call intercourse. This is all right when it happens between people who have fallen in love and gotten married. For that's the way the population of the world is kept up and actually increased year by year.

"But when it takes place between people who are not married, and who don't love each other, but are just 'out for a thrill,' it's something else again, for many reasons. The first is that it exposes both of them to very painful, serious, sometimes disgusting illnesses called venereal diseases–ask Bill whether he doesn't think this is reason enough to lay off that sort of stuff. But worse still–worse, because it's so rotten unfair–is the unwanted pregnancy that comes in spite of the precautions they told Bill were so sure. It's unfair because the girl gets so much worse a deal out of it than the boy does–though his share can be bad enough, if he has any decency at all about him.

"I needn't tell you what such a thing means to a girl. She is disgraced throughout the community, sometimes thrown out by her family, set aside as no longer fit for a decent man to marry. The boy who has caused all this must feel pretty terrible, even if it never comes out that he is the father of the child. For he has ruined the life and future prospects of a girl who was no more at fault than he was. Worst of all he has helped to send out into the world a poor little innocent kid that the law brands as illegitimate."

"But that's not justice," protested one of the boys.

"Who said it was just? I didn't–in fact, I just told you how rottenly unjust it is. But that's the way the world is set up, like it or not; and neither one person, nor yet a thousand who think they know better and would like to change things, can make it any different. So if you want to know who's really a poor sport, and about as low a louse as walks the earth, it's the fellow who does that miserable, cowardly thing to a girl for a few minutes or hours of so-called pleasure.

"Now let's shut up shop and get home and to bed, the whole lot of us. Glad you fellows felt like coming in and getting things straightened out. It reminds me of the days when I had a gang of Boy Scouts coming to the house to talk things over with the Scoutmaster; and later on, in the Army, when I was a Medical Officer and had to discuss these things with the men and officers in my command. It always helps to get things out into the open, instead of keeping them shut up and festering inside you.

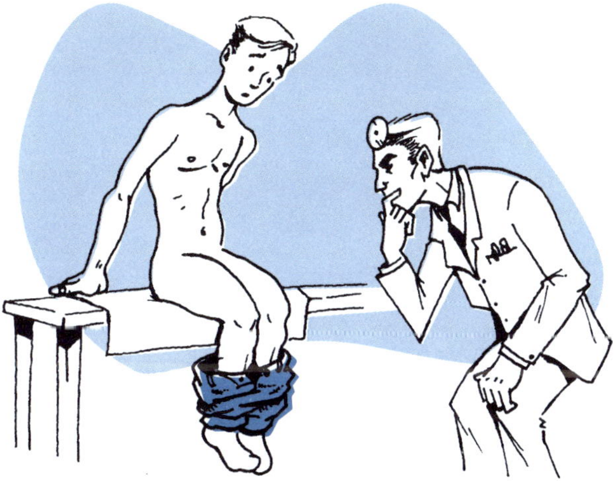

"It always helps to get things out into the open, instead of keeping them shut up and festering inside you."

"And Bill, you've had a very valuable lesson for free, take it from me. Next time you feel like taking a chance, remember how you felt between the time you had your fun–if you call it fun–and the time I told you you were okay and wouldn't have to pay for it this time. Then remember how good it felt to know that you were safe. It's worth thinking about, Bill. Goodnight!" and the boys walked off together, leaving the doctor to wonder how deep what he had been saying would sink in and bring the kind of results he hoped for.

Chapter 12

SPEEDING, AND BRAKES

"Have you seen Doc's new car?" asked Jim as he and Tom were passing the doctor's office. Just then the door opened to let out a patient, and the doctor, seeing the boys admiring his new car, beckoned them to come in.

"So you finally broke down and got that new bus, didn't you?" remarked Jim, as they entered the office. "It must have been a super salesman that persuaded you to turn in that faithful elderly contraption of yours."

"Yes, I must admit that he did do a little high pressure selling," conceded the doctor. "But if you think *he* was good, you should see the fuel salesman who's been trying to persuade me to use something they mix with the gas and grease. According to what he says, it must be the world's best."

"What does he claim for it?" asked the boys curiously.

"Well, for one thing, it makes the car go faster, so you can have a lot more fun with it. And it makes riding very much pleasanter and more comfortable, because you don't feel the bumps in the road. He says that many of the best people in town have been using it."

"Then what are you waiting for?" asked Jim. "If it's that good, I should think everybody would be using it."

"Lots of folks are. And he certainly makes out a good case for his product. But while I was being tempted to fall for his line, it suddenly occurred to me that there must be a gimmick in it somewhere. And sure enough, when I got him backed into a corner, he had to admit that there was one serious drawback and a few others that are nearly as bad."

"What was the big disadvantage?" the boys wanted to know.

"Why, it seems that the stuff somehow weakens your brakes so that they don't act quite so promptly, nor so efficiently, either. Then, too, if you once get used to using it, it's pretty hard to give it up; and the longer you use it, the more expensive it gets!"

"That sounds like a fairly long list of drawbacks," pondered Tom slowly. "Especially that business about the brakes. Would you dare to drive a car that didn't have a number one braking system?"

"Oh, I don't know if that means so much," replied the doctor. "He says some of the most careful and sensible men in town use it. If they can get by with it, why shouldn't I be able to? Besides, if you have more fun driving at the higher speeds it gives, why are the brakes so important?" and the doctor looked as if he wanted to be fair and hear both sides of the argument.

Both boys stared at him for almost a full minute. Their faces showed blank amazement. Finally Tom broke the silence.

"I don't mean any disrespect, doctor, honestly I don't. But you talk to me like someone who is slightly balmy. Do you actually expect us to believe that you, or any other sensible driver, would put a higher octane gas in your car, and at the same time weaken its braking equipment? I wonder if the salesman is telling the truth when he claims that sensible businessmen are mixing the stuff with their gas? I wouldn't drive round the block with you if I knew you had any of that bug juice in your tank. Would you, Jim?"

Jim gazed at the doctor thoughtfully, then shook his head in an emphatic negative, and spoke his mind forcefully.

"I don't want to hurt your feelings, Doc. But I wouldn't drive with you, or the most dependable driver I ever knew, who would do that fool stunt. I just wouldn't take that chance."

"I feel sure you *have* taken that chance, though, both of you, and many times too. And unless I am greatly mistaken, you'll do it a great many more times. I certainly hope you won't buy any of the stuff yourselves, though. And I hope the time may come when all of us will have sense enough not to use it, nor ride with people who do. Apparently, though, we are still a long way off from that good day."

"I can't believe the Government would allow such stuff to be sold," objected Jim stubbornly. "Why, it would be like carrying dynamite around on the public highway."

"But the Government does allow it. You see, they take in a lot of money on the tax, which is much higher than that on either plain or premium gas. I'll admit that lots of people think the Government could get its revenues in a lot of safer and more respectable ways. Still, they go on passing out the stuff just the same."

Suddenly Tom, who had been frowning perplexedly, broke into a loud horse laugh. Slapping Jim vigorously on the back, he shouted, "Haw, I get it. How about you, Jim, old scout?"

"What do you mean, 'you get it'? What do you get?"

"Wake up and think, Stupid. What do all the pious folks tell drivers not to mix with gasoline? What is it that makes driving more fun after you've drunk some of it? And what slows down your reflexes so that you can't tramp down on your brakes so quick? Come alive, Bird Brain," and Tom poked his friend vigorously in the ribs again.

"Well, I'm not going to preach a temperance sermon at you. But let's see if I've made any false claims about it. Let's take up the points one by one, and you can call me if I make a single statement that can't be proved by a dozen school textbooks and medical volumes, as well as pamphlets on safe driving.

"Alcohol, even the little bit there is in a cocktail or a glass of beer, slows down your judgment while it speeds up your emotions. So you drive faster, but much less carefully. By slowing down your reflexes, it lengthens the time it takes to apply brakes. It gets more expensive the longer you use it, because you get to taking more and more of it; and it's mighty hard to quit it once you get used to it. And you know as well as I do that not all the sensible business and professional men in town are on the wagon, though a lot of folks honestly believe the time will come when they'll have to get on board, or else stop driving while they drink.

"Remember, too, I'm not talking about drunken driving. It's the 'small one' that does all these dangerous things to the person who's driving and thinks he's as good as he is when he hasn't had that potent little bit of alcohol. You certainly have to admit that the Government does make a tidy sum taxing the stuff; though whether or not it's clear profit would take an accountant who would tot up injuries and deaths it causes against the financial intake.

"So think about what I've told you, next time you are taking a girl home from a party—especially if the lady of the house doesn't know what I've been talking about and has spiked the punch."

"But now that I've sold you my bill of goods, let's switch to one other thing about my magic juice. I mean what even a little bit of liquor, or even beer, does to the boy and girl after they've parked their car on a soft shoulder. Their emotions are heightened while their braking power (inhibitions, what the psychologist calls the good common sense that tells us to stop when we've gone far enough) is weakened. I don't need to tell you fellows that that adds up to a mighty dangerous combination.

"So think about what I've told you, next time you are taking a girl home from a party–especially if the lady of the house doesn't know what I've been talking about and has spiked the punch."

"You sure played us for suckers, Doc. You shouldn't have taken advantage of our tender years and your wisdom that has come from all the long years you've lived and charged people for your advice. That wasn't quite cricket, you know," and Tom looked doubtful, as though uncertain whether to kick himself, or reproach the doctor further.

"I'm sorry, fellows–honestly I am, and I humbly apologize. But you did look so trustful and so interested in my newly discovered devil juice that I just couldn't resist the temptation. But g'bye now; here comes a patient," and the doctor walked over to one door as the boys slipped out through the other.

Chapter 13

UNDERSTANDING YOURSELF

The doctor was taking his weekly afternoon off. He had invited his five friends to go along with him to the lake to try out his new speed boat and do a little fishing. Jim and Tom were working, but the others eagerly accepted.

The doctor had asked Harry to steer, so that he could lie back in the cockpit and relax. Just then something happened that completely killed any idea of relaxation he might have been indulging.

Another boat coming up from astern had tooted a raucous horn and then tried to cut across their bow. But the other skipper hadn't counted on Harry's adroitness, and still less on his quick temper. The angry boy jabbed the throttle wide open and shot ahead with a sudden burst of speed that threw his shipmates into a forcible huddle and banged Bill's head against Jack's with a resounding thump.

They barely cleared the other boat, and in doing so, just missed crashing through her shiny mahogany planking. Luckily for them all, Harry was able to get their own transom clear of the other's bow, but with what looked like hardly an inch margin. The other skipper cursed them heartily as he rocked in their wake.

"I bet he won't try that one again," chortled Harry, turning to the doctor for approval. Instead he met a cool, level look that pulled him up short. A look from the doctor always meant more to the boys than a tongue lashing from anyone else. So Harry at once launched into a defense of what he had done, winding up with:

"But you don't believe in a person's standing up for his rights, do you, sir?"

The doctor listened in silence until he had finished, then replied quietly:

"Stow it, Harry. I'd hoped maybe you'd grown up in this one respect, after your latest narrow squeak last week. But I guess you're one of those 'accident prone' people–the folks who never do grow up when it comes to driving or sailing. There are lots of men, yes, and women too, who are just kids when it comes to asserting their rights to the right of way.

"One of the things I'd hoped to talk to you fellows about at school was this business of understanding yourselves and what it is that makes you tick. I wanted to talk to you about the toughest job in the world–one that everybody has to learn to do, sooner or later, if he wants to save himself a lot of unnecessary grief.

"That job is learning to understand yourself, now that this change from boy into man has started."

"Well, take the wheel yourself if you think I'm too much of a kid to be trusted with this new battleship of yours. But honest, Doc, I won't do that fool trick again, or any other one either, I promise you, if you do let me keep on with her. But whether you do or not, I'd like to hear just what you would have told us at school, if there'd been time.

"We've still got most of the afternoon before us, and I'll keep her down to a comfortable pace, with no spasms of speed to teach other folks manners. That'll give us plenty of time."

Jack, who'd been wondering how the doctor would handle Harry's weakness as well as some others of his own, rubbed his aching forehead, and sat up alertly to listen, while Bill called back from where he was sitting in the bow:

"Don't pull any punches when you get round to my part of the sermon, Doc. I've told both Harry and Jack what a fool I made of myself the other night, and what I told you and what you told me. I can take anything; so don't mind my feelings."

"Right-o, then; carry on, Harry. We don't mind swimming to shore if we have to, just to prove what a devil of a man you are," and the doctor grinned as Harry winced at the dig he knew he had earned. "Let's forget it. But I would like to tell you–"

"Excuse me, Doc. But can you really tell me why do you sup pose it is that I do these fool stunts," interrupted Harry. "I swear every time I won't do this sort of thing again–and I mean it at the time. But I get so cussing mad when someone tries to put one over on me, that it seems as if I just *have* to show him that I'm as good as he is–and maybe just a little bit better!" and Harry unconsciously shrugged back his shoulders and sat up a little bit straighter as he remembered how he had wiped the other fellow's eye by his sudden tack and spurt.

"Why, Harry, you've just told us why; but not by your words. It's your actions that give you away," laughed the doctor. "You don't realize it, but you're just like every other Joe your age in not feeling quite sure how good you are. That means that you have to take every chance you get to show what a man you are! And you underline this thing you're not sure of by sticking out your chest and straightening your back, as you did just now.

"No, I don't mean that you want to show *me*. It's the other fellows, as well as yourself, you've got to prove it to. By the time you get to be my age, you'll know perfectly well that you are not so hot, as every one does sooner or later who isn't a stuffed shirt who's succeeded in fooling himself. And by that time you'll realize what a waste of time it is to try to convince yourself and your pals of something you know just isn't so. Sounds sort of screwy, doesn't it? But it happens to be the truth.

"And besides, just now, it isn't nearly so important to you what *I* think about you, or what your dad or your mother or your teachers or any other old timers like us prehistoric dodoes (yes, I know that's what you think we are) believe about you. Forget it, Bill," (as the older boy started to interrupt) "You don't have to be polite and tactful. I know you fellows think I'll be passing out in a few short years.

"What really rates with all you fellows is what other lads your own age, and even more those who are just a little older than you are, think about how good you are. Harry tries to prove it by beating the other car, or boat. Guys from the wrong side of the railroad track sometimes try to do it by smashing windows, or breaking into a house, or releasing the brakes or slashing the tires of parked cars.

"Hot rods, and motorcyclists–no matter what their age is in years–are just as far from being grown up. Their jalopies or their stripped-down motors or their fire-cracker-popping motorcycles are to build them up with their own crowd–and with anyone else on the road that they can impress with their show-off antics.

"What determines the particular variety of kid tricks a fellow indulges in isn't so much a matter of his own choice as it is what the rest of his crowd considers he-man stuff. With nine- or ten-year-olders, it may be writing dirty words on the walls of the school toilets. With thirty- or forty-year-old sex offenders who aren't any more than ten years old emotionally, it may be whispering dirty suggestions to others like themselves or to innocent kids they can get hold of."

Harry suddenly interrupted, with what was apparently a new idea that had just dawned on him.

"Do you suppose that could be why the Bat Fraternity has those wild hazings and dangerous initiations, the kind that killed that little freshman last year, and nearly broke up the frat? You certainly don't believe that *those* fellows, who every one in school knows are stuck on themselves because they've been tapped by the best and most exclusive club in school–it couldn't be that *they* aren't dead sure of themselves, could it?" and Harry looked as if he just couldn't swallow *that* idea.

"Of course they're not sure of themselves, Harry, any more than you are, or Jack is, or Bill. Just what is a snob, and why is

"What determines the particular variety of kid tricks a fellow indulges in isn't so much a matter of his own choice as it is what the rest of his crowd considers he-man stuff. With nine- or ten-year-olders, it may be writing dirty words on the walls of the school toilets."

he, anyway, do you suppose? Or didn't you ever stop to wonder? Well, I'll tell you; and then you try it out on your friends, and see if I'm not right.

"A snob is a person who isn't sure of how he stands with other people, and so low-rates everybody but those he considers his superiors. In this way he tries to make himself feel that he must be better than those who want his approval, and so he hurts them and humiliates them to assure himself of his power over them. When he blackballs a fraternity candidate or turns down an applicant for membership in his 'exclusive' club, he thinks he's showing how much better man he is than the poor helpless boob he's excluding. For every snob has a good bit of the bully in him, you see.

"Another thing younger fellows are nuts about is the approval of Joes a little older than themselves, though not old enough to be nearing the grave, like their dads or uncles or myself. That's one reason so many fellows pet and even go the limit with girls. It's not for any pleasure or satisfaction they get out of it themselves, but just to show the girls, and other fellows who are the least little bit older, that they are perfectly normal and masculine."

Here Bill, who had been listening with the closest attention, suddenly cut in:

"Do you know, Doc, that's exactly what was eating on me the other night when I was out with those older guys and got myself into the spot I was so tense about when I came to your office. *I* didn't really want to have anything to do with that skirt. As a matter of fact, she was actually sort of disgusting to me. But I didn't want the others to think there was anything wrong with me, or that I was 'queer,' or that I couldn't rate with the rest of them.

"So I just went ahead and acted like a fool. And all I got out of what I see now was just a fool stunt was several days of sure-enough mental hell, before you told me I hadn't caught any disease but was just imagining things. A dollar will get you five that I won't be *that* sort of a come-on again," and Bill slid back down on the bottom of the boat with a sigh of relief at the mere recollection of his escape from his little private Hades.

"I hate 'dating,'" volunteered Jack, hesitantly. "But it sure does buck me up to have the other fellows hear girls I've been around with say I've got a cute line, or that I'm no peasant for a tot my size. It really builds me," and Jack, who had been listening in silence up to now, stuck out his chin with a pleased expression of self-satisfaction at what he considered his "sharp" vocabulary, then added:

"But I sure straighten up and die when a deep-pocket wipes me just because he has a big car."

"Deflate, hub cap. Stop acting so sophisticated, and talk plain American," and Harry shoved the subdued Jack over on the thwart with his elbow, then remarked thoughtfully: "I wonder if you can't help me with something else that's bothering me–"

"Maybe so, maybe so, Harry. But first, Jack, get forward and cut up some of that bait, and break out the fishing tackle, will you, Bill? And for Pete's sake, Harry, give me a crack at that wheel! I brought you loafers along to act as a crew, not for a lot of passengers to keep me from having a little bit of fun myself with my own ship. Get going, sailor," and the doctor pushed Harry to one side, took over the wheel, and gave her the gun. As soon as she reached full speed, he threw the helm over with a flourish, putting her into a tight turn.

Unfortunately for him and his dignity, he had completely failed to notice a very small dinghy at mooring that lay directly in their way as they rounded a point. The skidding speed boat would most certainly have demolished her had it not been for the quick thinking and fast action of Bill and Harry.

Bill grabbed the boat hook and Harry snatched up a paddle, and between them they succeeded in fending off the dinghy, though she scraped a wide strip of paint off their shiny white side as they shot past her. They all watched her intently as she bobbed crazily up and down in their wake. Then the boys looked at one another in dead silence, but grinning broadly with no attempt to conceal their feelings.

The doctor had the grace to flush guiltily, then looked around sheepishly, to meet the level gaze of Harry, who did his very best to give him the cool, rather scornful look that had gone in the opposite direction earlier in the afternoon, when another collision had been averted. Then he relaxed and chuckled, while the rest of the boys howled with laughter at the doctor's humiliation.

The next minute they had reached the float and were tumbling helter-skelter out of the boat and up the steep bank. The doctor followed them, considerably subdued by this chagrin over the narrow escape he had not deserved after his lubberly trick. They had almost reached the top of the back when Harry remarked, condescendingly:

"Don't feel too bad about it, Doc. The best of us have to show off sometimes, and come a cropper while doing so," then tripped and fell flat on his face as the doctor's foot shot out and caught him unawares.

"Don't forget the respect due to old age, pal," grinned the doctor, and the account was balanced and closed to the satisfaction of all concerned.

Chapter 14

GETTING ALONG WITH DAD

Supper was over, the frying pan, tin plates and cups had been hastily scraped and dunked by Jack, the rookie of the crew; and the embers over which they had cooked the fish and boiled the coffee had been replenished with driftwood to make a roaring blaze.

The boys were gathered round it chatting over the day's events. But the talk gradually died down, as the glowing coals took the place of the roaring flames and cast flickering shadows that lighted the serious faces of the group. Suddenly Bill reached over and poked Harry none too gently in the ribs:

"Wake up, sourball. What's all the gloom about? You look as if you'd swallowed the anchor when we came ashore, instead of dropping it. Tell Papa all your little troubles."

Without deigning to give so much as a glance in Bill's direction, Harry studied the fire a minute or two longer in silence, then turned slowly toward the doctor. "How about doing like you promised you would and telling me what makes me feel the way I do about my dad? When I was younger, I always used to think he was the biggest of the big shots. But now–"

"Well, just how *do* you feel about him now, Harry?" asked the doctor.

"Why, I admire him a lot, more than any other man I know, I guess. He can hire or fire a man, or close a deal, or make rattling good after-dinner talk with the best of them. Besides, he gives me almost anything I want, though he does make me mad by asking me unnecessary questions about why I want it, and what I do with it after he gives it to me.

"But he gets me all mixed up. And I believe he's just about as confused about me as I am about myself. One minute he lets me drive one of the cars, even though he knows it's against the law because I'm not old enough. I'm big for my age, so everyone who sees me driving thinks I'm a lot older. Then the very next day he'll bawl me out because I use my own judgment and buy a tie he doesn't think is so hot, or make a decision about something he thinks I'm too much of a kid to be trusted with making.

"Besides, he nags me and says I'm breaking the law when I drive 65 or a little bit over. Yet he'll push the new Cadillac up to 85 and higher, and then say it's no matter about a fool law because it's perfectly safe on a straightaway–and there's no highway patrolman in sight! I'd just love to see him pinched–no, I guess I wouldn't, really, though it would sure serve him good and right," and Harry shook his head uncertainly and ran his hands through his hair as though he just couldn't make sense of it all.

"Why, I admire him a lot, more than any other man I know, I guess. He can hire or fire a man, or close a deal, or make rattling good after-dinner talk with the best of them."

The doctor sat quietly thinking for a full minute, then began: "One of the hardest things for a boy to take is for his father to treat him in the confusing way you speak of, Harry. That is, expecting him one minute to act like a mature man, and panning him the next minute for acting as a man would. At the same time, that's the very hardest thing for a father *not* to do!

"But it isn't so strange that a dad finds some difficulty in deciding the tricky question of how far along you are in the scale of development, when you don't know yourself just where you stand. And I can tell you that that's the case with every normal boy, and not with you alone.

"So instead of asking your dad to be patient with you, I'm going to reverse the usual order by putting in a plug for him and asking *you* to try to be patient with *him*! Just do your best, all of you, to be kind to us old birds, and overlook our blunders when we treat you like kids where we ought to treat you like men. And try your best not to expect us to treat you like men and expect more from you than you are grown up enough to put across. Don't blame us too much when we forget for a minute that you are not still the kids you were just a few years ago!"

"But dad can act like a sure-enough pain in the neck at times," argued Jack.

"Admitted. But you youngsters aren't exactly soothing to the neck, yourselves, at times. So try to have a heart, will you?

"As to your dad, Harry, I know and you know that he isn't perfect, and he knows it too, though you'd better not tell him so if you know what's good for you. No father is, for that matter; I know I wasn't with my sons. But as far as I'm concerned, I shouldn't want to have a dad that was perfect, and I don't believe you would, either. Yet from what you yourself have just told us, and from what I've seen of him, he must be a pretty good egg. Anyway, I happen to know that he's a heap sight better father than those of a number of boys I know. And that goes for your dad, Bill, and for yours too, Jack.

"So why not take him for what he is, just as we all have to get along with the folks we're brought into contact with in business or social life or school? When he tells you to do what you both know is right, do it, not because it's what he tells you to do, but because it's right, or the law, or what decent folks naturally do.

"When he does something you don't think is quite right, or asks you to do something you don't think he's justified in asking of you, don't argue or fuss at the time if you don't want to catch a cyclone. Then some time later, be man enough and frank enough to ask his reason for what he did, or asked you to do. Say that you're not criticizing him, but that you are honestly interested in knowing.

"It may be a little hard for him to take, at first; but I know your father pretty well, and I've seen him in some pretty tough spots. I believe that if you'll treat him in this adult way, just as you would treat another man whether of his age or yours, you'll be surprised at the way your relations will improve.

"I know I've had a lot to learn in dealing with my sons. It's hard for us to remember that we were kids too, just as you used to be; but that you and we both have grown up. And you can help us with this tough job of learning to treat you as men and not like the little fellows we used to boss, if you'll remember to try to act like men. We never did own you, even in those days that are gone. We certainly don't own you now."

"Any suggestions as to how I might start?" queried Harry, with the air of someone who was willing to take a chance on anything that seemed reasonable.

"Well, one way would be to make up your mind not to take the opposite side of every question he happens to be discussing at the table or when you happen to have company. It's a big temptation, I know, but so is monkeying with a buzz saw. I don't mean never to express an honest opinion, nor to agree with everything he says. That would be bootlicking, and that wouldn't help.

"What I mean is to try to see things through the other fellow's eyes, even if the other fellow happens to be your dad. That's good practice for debating. See how it works at home.

"Then, too, it's a good idea to mention something good you may have heard someone say about him. That's not flattery. It's just one of the pleasant things you can do to make life run more smoothly. You'll be surprised at the way he'll take that.

"Still another thing you'd probably never think of doing is mentioning some good looking suit of clothes, or a snappy tie, or a becoming hat, when he first puts them on. You don't have to make up compliments. Just say what you think and feel when it happens to be on the good side. (Take my advice though and keep mum if you think they make him look like something the cat dragged in. That can happen sometimes with us old fellows when we try to dress like one of the boys!) These are all little things, I know. But I know you'll be more than pleased at the way they oil up some of the creaking squeaking spots in the family's daily goings on. One more tip, though. Don't say one of these nice things just before you touch him for a five spot."

The fire was almost out. There was silence. Somehow it didn't seem the time for any more talk. It was time to break camp–and to think some long thoughts. The doctor tossed a bucket of water on the embers, and the boys stamped out the last glowing coals among the ashes. The doctor broke the silence.

"Now pack up the duffel, make everything snug and shipshape, and let's get going. The last one in the car is a rot–"

"Careful, Doc; no coarse language!" and Jack ducked adroitly as the doctor shied a chunk of firewood at him. Then they filed down the bank in silence, each doing a lot of thinking.

Chapter 15

AN AGE-OLD QUESTION

The doctor had invited some of the fellows to one of his one-night-a-month fireside parties where they sat around the big log fire and got off their chests some of the things boys talk about and worry over. "One of the doc's get-togethers is better than any high school bull session we ever have," Tom had confided to a friend once. "You can ask that guy *anything*–nothing you say ever gets him ruffled, he tells you what you want to know, and nobody else ever hears anything about it."

They had been talking over the team's record for the past year, and prospects for the year ahead, and the talk had come round, as it so often does these days, to the question of professionalism in sports, and what is permitted and what is frowned on. After each one had had his say and the doctor had summed up the sentiment of the group, they fell silent. The lights hadn't been lighted, and only the occasional flare-up of a burning log lit up a thoughtful face here and there round the circle.

At last Bill broke the silence. "It seems to me, doctor, that in all these questions of what's right and what's wrong–athletics, relations with girls, cheating at exams, the honor system, and all the rest of it–it's always the 'don'ts' and never the 'do's' that you moralists keep harping on–"

"Hold it, Bill," the doctor interrupted. "Why do you call me a moralist? And have you ever heard me 'harp' on anything, or rub in what *I* think you ought to do about anything you ask me about?"

"You know he doesn't, Bill," broke in two or three of the group. And Jim continued, "He just gives it to us straight and lets us make up our own minds what we want to do in the spot that we happen to be in and that we're batting our gums over," and Jim looked around belligerently as if to challenge anyone to dispute his defense of their friend.

"Oh yes, I know, I know," retorted Bill a little shortly. "You don't have to defend Doc to me, any of you. But what I mean is, he's always on what folks that are older and supposed to be wiser than we are, think is the right side of the argument, whatever it happens to be. And even though he may not say so in so many words, he always lets us see what he thinks we *ought* to do and hopes we *will* do, without telling us we *have* to do it.

"What I want to know is this. Why is it that the thing a fellow wants to do because it's fun and enjoyable is always the wrong thing that folks disapprove of, while the thing they want us to do, and Doc wants us to do, too, is pretty dull milksop sort of stuff. Don't you see what I mean, sir?" and Bill stopped, as if he knew he hadn't yet made himself clear, though he was sure of his ground.

The others looked uncertain. They didn't want to seem disloyal to their older friend, yet they realized that Bill had touched on something that had puzzled and bothered each one of them when he had had a tough decision to make.

The doctor frowned as he studied the fire–then looked up relieved, and smiled. "Bill's got something there," he said slowly, as if groping for words with which to express what he was thinking. "Come to think of it, the things I've told you *have* been sort of cold oatmeal, haven't they?

"So often the things folks tell us *not* to do seem so much more fun than what we're told we *ought* to do, that going straight looks like a pretty sad sack sort of a show. The ministers, the Scout leaders, the Sunday School teachers, those of us who really like boys, even the best of us seem to be fighting a losing fight. We always seem to be stopping fellows from doing the things they want to do and that they feel sure will be good fun, and urging them to do stuff that is as dull as dishwater," and he rubbed his forehead perplexedly.

Suddenly he straightened up in his chair, then leaned forward and gave the fire a vigorous jab with the poker. It sent the sparks flying up the chimney, and started a blaze that lit up his face, as well as those of the rest of the circle. "Men, I believe I've got something!"

The boys looked at him expectantly, then Jim popped out with the word that most of them had been thinking:

"Give!"

"All right, then. You asked for it. Here it is. If you get tired listening, just holler 'Uncle' and I'll quit.

"You all know, of course, that what Bill has just stumbled on is a bit of philosophizing that is as old as the hills. Folks, whether they're old or young, have always thought that the thing they want to do *right now* is the thing that's the most fun; while the thing that has to be put off till tomorrow or next year isn't worth thinking about, or planning for, or giving up anything for. And that anyone who urges you to wait or save up for the future is an old fuddy duffy that wants to cheat you out of the good times you're entitled to.

"The old wheeze, 'Let's eat and drink today, for tomorrow we die,' is one way of expressing it. Another is 'Tomorrow's a long way off–this is today.' Still another one is: 'You're only young once–better have a good time while you can.'

"One trouble with that philosophy is that 'today' is over so quickly–and then comes the 'tomorrow' that seemed so far off. So if you've had for only today what tasted or felt or looked good, and have spoiled things for tomorrow when you'll be every bit as anxious for good things as you are today, you've made kind of a fool of yourself. For 'today' is never very long in passing, while there'll be a lot of tomorrows, and tomorrows, and tomorrows that will be pretty dull, if you've used up all your fun today.

"The other trouble is that so often the thing that everyone thinks is going to be so much fun, that it's worth sacrificing tomorrow for it, turns out not to be much fun after all. Somehow you just can't make me believe you think it's always more fun to act like a heel than it is to be a good sport and do the square-shooting thing.

"Do you really mean to tell me that there is any one of you here who would actually have more pleasure doing something that you knew would ruin the whole future of a girl you like, respect and have had good times with, than in acting in such a way as to make it possible for those good times to continue? Maybe some day marrying her, if you haven't changed in your feelings toward her in the meantime; or, if you have, seeing her marry some good friend of yours?

"Which would give you more real honest-to-goodness satisfaction–fun, if you prefer to call it that? Acting decent and enjoying every minute of the time you spend with the girl? Or taking her off to some greasy-spoon, juke-box-blaring, hole-in-the-wall beer joint, or sitting for hours in a parked car and doing something you and the girl would both be ashamed of the next day, and the day after that, and every future day you had to live?

"It looks to me as if you'd have to have more 'fun' in one night than I've ever known of anybody's having to outweigh and overbalance the rotten feelings a decent guy would have all the rest of his born days, for having done a thing like that.

"Some time, make the experiment of asking a man with a bad hangover whether the fun he had getting that way the night before makes up for the rotten hours of the following day. No, that's not preaching; it's plain common sense.

"How much respect would your dad get from you–and I happen to know from experience that having his son's respect is something a man thinks a lot of–if he wasn't willing to deny himself some fun so as to take out insurance for your mother, or put some money in the bank for your education? I'll venture that the father of every one of you gets more actual satisfaction out of looking at his insurance policy or totting up his bank account than he'd get out of horsing around in a sporty convertible. And you know as well as I do how touchy they are about the cars they drive, to say nothing of those they would

"I'll venture that the father of every one of you gets more actual satisfaction out of looking at his insurance policy or totting up his bank account than he'd get out of horsing around in a sporty convertible."

be driving if they weren't thinking more of tomorrow's good times than they are of today's.

"You know these dads of yours aren't pious or noble. They don't feel self-righteous, either. They're just looking ahead for their satisfaction."

"Oh, come on now, Doc," objected Harry disgustedly. "Do you honestly expect us to believe it's more fun to be a goody-goody sad sack than to do a little necking after a party?" and he looked round the circle for backing. "Or to spout 'The lips that touch wine shall never touch mine' when a good looker offers you a glass of spiked punch at a dance? Or to come home and be able to look your mother in the eye and say, 'Mamma, I've been your good little boy all evening. Aren't you proud of me?' Bah! Phooey!" and Harry spat in the fire to show his disgust at the mere idea.

"Don't ask me, Harry," countered the doctor good-naturedly. "Don't ask the other fellows, either. Just ask yourself. And don't tell me the answer, either. If you can convince yourself it was more fun to eat all that rich stuff when you lost your place on the track team for breaking training before last year's meet, than it would have been to be one of the men who won the interscholastic championship, go right ahead. But I don't believe you can make it stick.

"If you can, then you're a lot different stuff from most of our best ball players and track men. *They* don't call it 'preaching' or 'moralizing' when coach expects them to give up today's fun for tomorrow's 'win' and the celebration that goes along with it. And I don't believe *you* do, either.

"How much did you enjoy your fun the other night, Bill? 'Tomorrow' came mighty soon for you, didn't it? And if you'd contracted the bad luck you thought you had, it would have proved the most expensive fun you'd ever had."

"Heck, it wasn't fun even while I was doing it. I told you that," admitted Bill disgustedly.

"No, and the same way with Harry's 'not being goody-goody.' You see–"

"Excuse me for interrupting, doctor," interposed Tom, rather hesitantly. "But what's that purring sound? It sounds to me like–"

"It sounds to me like adenoids, men," shouted Jim from the other end of the circle, with a loud laugh. "Stop that snoring and wake up, little man. It's time for 'itta boys to be tucked in bed. But we'll take good care of you, never fear," and he and Bill dragged poor Jack into the light of the fire. There he stumbled about, rubbing his eyes, while the older boys shouted with laughter and pushed him none too gently hither and yon in the flickering light. The doctor's talk ended abruptly.

"You'll have to excuse us, Doc. But you can see for yourself what a long, dull sermon can do to even a highly intelligent congregation," and Jim grinned his widest grin.

"Off with you, the whole kit and b'ilin of you. And don't come around here again inviting me to cast pearls before you swi–you gentlemen," and the doctor got to his feet in mock indignation. "Time to go on home, and see if you can't repent of your lack of respect for my bald gray hairs. Next meeting will be at the lake," and the boys trooped out of the house and down the steps, laughing and talking as they went. The doctor turned back and sat down before the fire, poking it into flames again.

Chapter 16

SO LONG, FELLOWS

To the fellows who've stuck it out and finished reading this book for the first time:

Most books start with a dedication to someone the writer likes and admires and wants to honor. This one goes at things the other way round, for it ends with a dedication.

But it is like other books in one way. It is dedicated to some people the writer likes and admires, and would like to honor–if he thought they'd let him get away with it and not razz him for doing it.

These people are the Harrys, Jacks, Jims, Toms and Bills he has known, and liked, and admired, and worked with, and had good times with through the years. A few of them, a very few, are older than he is; a lot more are his own age, while more, far more, of them are a good bit younger.

If you've read this book through, you've learned something about how boys and men are made, and in what ways they are different from girls and women. And you've learned, too, that there is quite a bit to this growing up business that everyone just has to go through.

There's something else that you may not believe just yet, but you will come to believe it later on. And that is that to most men, growing up completely means, sooner or later, getting married and having boys, and perhaps girls, of their own. Men and women who don't do this usually seem to feel, as they get on in life, that they've missed some of the very best things life might have given them.

"... to most men, growing up completely means, sooner or later, getting married and having boys, and perhaps girls, of their own. Men and women who don't do this usually seem to feel, as they get on in life, that they've missed some of the very best things life might have given them."

How can you tell that? Well, just look around you at the people you know and respect, the people you hear about over the radio, see in the current events in the movies or on television, or read about in the papers. Just about every one of them is married; see if they're not. And the time will come when even Jack here, who is so sure of himself now, will tumble, just as most other normal men do.

When that time comes, you are going to be mighty glad you did the right thing, the square thing, the thing you knew was what you ought to do. You're going to be "grown up" a long time. So if you know that what you are doing now is going to contribute to your self-respect and your good health and that of those you love for all those long years ahead, you can get a lot of satisfaction even now in knowing that you are storing up good times instead of bad for yourself in the years to come.

There's something more you've learned about growing up, if you didn't know it before, something that some folks never seem to learn. And that is that growing up isn't something any one can do, like rolling off a log. It takes effort, and plenty of it.

Maybe this book will help you handle some of the difficult things that happen while you're growing up. Maybe it will make it easier for you to understand what it is that makes you feel and think and act the way you do. And maybe it will help you *not* to do some of the things many fellows do hastily, and thoughtlessly, without the slightest idea of the consequences that may not show up until long afterwards–and then regret them for the rest of their lives. For these early mistakes that seem so unimportant have a way of sticking to a fellow the way a burr sticks to a long-haired dog; he just can't seem to shake them off.

And yet, although growing up can be such a difficult, unpleasant, tough job that often throws a fellow completely off balance for a while, it can be a time when he feels pretty good, sometimes so good that it seems as if he could lick the whole world. Maybe this book has helped you feel that way, too.

But every book has got to end sometime, and this one must, too. So it's just:

"So long, fellows, I'll be seeing you–I hope!"

For GIRLS ONLY

For GIRLS ONLY

The Doctor Discusses the Mysteries of Womanhood

DR. FRANK HOWARD RICHARDSON

HOW BOOKS
Cincinnati, Ohio
www.howdesign.com

 Published by HOW Books, an imprint of F+W Publications, Inc., 4700 East Galbraith Road, Cincinnati, Ohio 45236. (800) 289-0963. First edition.

For more fine books from F+W Publications, visit www.fwbookstore.com.

11 10 09 08 07 5 4 3 2 1

Distributed in Canada by Fraser Direct, 100 Armstrong Avenue, Georgetown, Ontario, Canada L7G 5S4, Tel: (905) 877-4411. Distributed in the U.K. and Europe by David & Charles, Brunel House, Newton Abbot, Devon, TQ12 4PU, England, Tel: (+44) 1626 323200, Fax: (+44) 1626 323319, E-mail: postmaster@davidandcharles.co.uk. Distributed in Australia by Capricorn Link, P.O. Box 704, Windsor, NSW 2756 Australia, Tel: (02) 4577-3555.

Library of Congress Cataloging-in-Publication Data

Richardson, Frank Howard, 1882-
For boys only : the doctor discusses the mysteries of manhood; and, For girls only : the doctor discusses the mysteries of womanhood / Frank Howard Richardson.
p. cm.
ISBN 978-1-60061-069-1 (pbk. : alk. paper)
1. Sex instruction for boys. 2. Sex instruction for girls. I. Richardson, Frank Howard, 1882- For girls only. II. Title. III. Title: For girls only.
HQ41.R485 2007
612.6--dc22 2007034837

Edited by Amy Schell
Designed by Grace Ring
Illustrated by Greg Nock

F+W PUBLICATIONS, INC.

ABOUT THE AUTHOR

Dr. Frank Howard Richardson was educated in the United States (Cornell University) and in Europe (Vienna and Berlin). He was a pediatrician certified by the American Board of Pediatrics, and was a member of the American Academy of Pediatrics, The American College of Physicians, the Southern Medical Association and the American Medical Association. He was a lecturer and well-known writer, having contributed to leading medical journals and popular magazines. He is the author of ten books: *For Boys Only, For Girls Only, Simplifying Motherhood, Parenthood and the Newer Psychology, Rebuilding the Child, The Nervous Child and His Parents, The Pre-School Child and His Posture* (with Winifred J. Hearn), *Feeding Our Children, Letters From a Doctor to Expectant Parents*, and *The Nursing Mother: A Handbook on Breast Feeding*. He was also the father of two daughters and three sons.

Table Of

CONTENTS

FOREWORD

When I was about five years old, my mother sat me down on the end of her bed and tried to explain "the birds and the bees" in terms that I'd understand. What I came away with was that a mommy and a daddy climbed into bed and went to sleep. Sometime during the night, tiny sperm would march out of the daddy (I wasn't sure from where), cross the bed and climb into the mommy. Somehow the sperm would find an egg, break into it and turn it into a baby.

It wasn't until she gave me a book called *Where Did I Come From*, a few years later, that I finally began to understand how it really works. The book included a cartoon drawing of a chubby couple in bed. I'm pretty sure the daddy was on top. "Oh," I said, as a light bulb went on in my head, "that makes much more sense than tiny sperm walking across a huge bed."

When I was maybe eight years old, my mother presented me with another book by the same author called *What's Happening to Me?*, which explained the mysteries of puberty. I remember looking at a drawing of a girl examining her growing chest and peeking down my own shirt to see what was going on down there.

I was young enough when my parents decided I should learn about the facts of life, that I took it rather seriously. If they'd waited a few more years, I would have been embarrassed by the whole thing. After that, the topic wasn't raised again until I went to college.

During the long drive to freshman orientation, my father tried to tell me something important. "You know, you'll want to be careful. If you go to parties and there's drinking, you should make sure not to get too drunk and stick with your friends. You know, don't go anywhere alone."

I wasn't quite sure what he was trying to say, besides, "Don't get drunk." During the orientation, one of the campus safety officers addressed the issue of date rape. My father leaned over and whispered, "That's what I was talking about."

"Really, could have fooled me," I thought to myself.

But my dad was certainly not alone in his inability to talk frankly about sex with me, which is why every generation has its own facts-of-life handbook that parents can give to their kids to avoid the awkward conversation (but still feel like they're doing a good job).

In fact, my mother once showed me the book that my grandmother had given her when she was about twelve years old. The small white pamphlet included lovely line illustrations and ridiculous advice like: Don't shower during menstruation, as you might catch a chill. And don't over-exert yourself with activities like swimming or horseback riding.

So when I came across a book called *For Boys Only: The Doctor Discusses the Mysteries of Manhood* in a dusty used

bookstore, I happily paid a dollar for it and took my treasure home to peruse. First published in 1952, *For Boys Only* presents sex ed, health and dating advice in the form of a story. "Real" boys talk about girls and ask questions of a trusted local doctor who answers them frankly. I have one word for you: hilarious.

The book's back cover included a mention of another title called *For Girls Only,* and I immediately knew I had to find that book, too. Luckily, we live in the era of eBay, and it only took me a few tries to track down a copy. True to form, it was just as side-splittingly funny as the boys book.

As I read through both books (and marked my favorite passages), I started to wonder if the teenagers of the 1950s found these books just as amusing as I did...

The year is 1952. You're sitting on your bed painting your toenails when your mother appears in the doorway. "Dear," she says, with a serious tone in her voice. "I have something important to give you."

You glance up to see that your mother is holding a slim volume and resolutely handing it to you. "So, if you have any questions about the monthly curse and going steady with boys, my friend Mrs. Whitman says that this will have the answers. It helped her daughter a great deal when she was your age."

"Yes, mother," you say with a polite smile, taking the book and placing it on your night table.

But I could just as easily imagine the same thing happening in 1975.

You're sitting on your bed sorting through your sticker collection. "Honey," your mother says, appearing in your doorway. "I've got a little something here for you. Maggy next door says it helped her daughter understand the mysteries of her moon time and how to handle boys."

Or 2008, as you're sitting on your bed texting a friend. "Sweetie," your mother says, which she only calls you when you're in trouble or she has to give you some bad news. "I'm sure you have some questions about getting your period and hanging out with boys, and I haven't been around much lately to answer them. But I picked this book up at the airport and I think you'll get a lot out of it."

Eventually, you'd pick up the book and flip through the pages. A few fun words like *sex, breasts* and *heavy petting* would stand out and you'd start to read. But once you'd gotten through a few chapters, you'd begin to realize that while the book offered a few clues about the impending changes of puberty, it revealed much more about your parents and what their generation believed about sex and growing up.

And no matter what year it was, you'd know in your heart that they didn't have a clue.

So without further ado, we present in its entirety, *For Girls Only—The Doctor Discusses the Mysteries of Womanhood.*

Enjoy!
Megan Lane Patrick
Editor

Chapter 1

WHAT DO GIRLS TALK ABOUT?

"Mary Ann just makes me sick the way she flounces around at school as if she owned the universe."

"Yes, she gives me a pain, too. I can't stand the way she fixes her hair as if she were sixteen years old. She's big enough to be twenty, but she's only fourteen. And have you noticed the lipstick she puts on? My mother would have a fit if I ever looked like that. I have to buy my lipstick without her knowing it and put it on at school."

The two girls, Helen and Nell, had been sitting at a table in the corner drug store, sipping a soft drink from a bottle. They had started to get up, when who should walk in but Mary Ann and Jack. The girls instantly sat back in their chairs, played with their bottles, and pretended to look the other way.

"Speaking of angels," Helen whispered.

"Or should I say devils?" Nell muttered.

"Doesn't she think she is wonderful having a date? She acts as if she owned him, but I saw Jack yesterday with Betty and the day before with Jane. Mary Ann needn't act as if she were the only one."

Mary Ann and Jack sat at the counter. Each ordered a soda bulging with ice cream, completely ignoring Helen and Nell. The girls had seen enough, so they decided it was time to go, but as Helen passed behind them, she could not resist the temptation of catching her foot, which was none too dainty, in Mary Ann's stool, almost knocking her over.

When out on the street of their little town, they decided to go to the post office and pick up the mail and then walk by the ball field and watch their team practice. There was almost a feeling of summer in the air. It was time to be thinking about going to camp soon. Both girls had gone the previous year and were planning to return. Mary Ann was going also, but for the first time. They still could not get her out of their minds. Somehow she had gotten under their skin.

"Well, I know one thing. When Mary Ann gets to camp, she's going to have some of that stuck-up air knocked out of her. I can hardly wait for a swimming meet or tennis match. I *know* I can beat her all to pieces."

Helen added: "Yes, and I bet she doesn't know how to handle a canoe either. Then she will not be holding her nose in the air as if she were so much better than we are. And there will be no boys there, either, for her to try to show off before. I can hardly wait for camp to open. By the way, did you know that Lady is going to speak before the Woman's Club sometime

this summer? She is going to tell our mothers all about everything–what the camp stands for, what we do and–"

"And," added Nell with a laugh, "what our mothers are *not* to send us–a big box of candy or an enormous cake. Will you ever forget when Betty was sent all those goodies from home? Lady would not let her have them, but made her divide them all at dinner time. But, do you know, she was a good sport about it! Anyhow, just looking at Lady makes you want to do the right thing. She is so wonderful, and isn't she beautiful?"

"I can see her now in that gorgeous blue dress, the night of the banquet. I wish I could be just like her when I grow up."

As they were approaching the ball field, a car honked and stopped. It was Helen's mother.

"Girls, don't you want to hop in and go for a ride? I have some marketing to do; and if you like, you can choose what you want for supper. If it's sausage and pancakes, you may take over as cooks. I'll telephone Mrs. Brower, and I am sure she will let Nell stay for supper. We might ask Jane and Mary Ann too," but in unison both girls put thumbs down on Mary Ann. Mrs. Brown wisely did not ask for the reasons they did not want to ask their old friend with whom they had played since the first grade.

The three girls prepared the supper. As a surprise for Mr. and Mrs. Brown, they had bought a few extras in the way of nuts, as well as a package of marshmallows to toast in front of the open fire.

And so, with the dishes washed, the girls squatted in front of the fireplace with their long forks. Mrs. Brown had left the

room, so they felt as free to talk as if they were at school. But she was only in the next room, and she could hear pretty well what was going on. She heard Helen say:

"Oh, I wish school were not going to close quite yet. I just hate to think that I won't see Miss Cooper again for all summer. I did not expect to like algebra; but I studied my head off, just to have her give me one of her smiles."

"I wonder why she never married," added Jane. "You know, she's old. She's twenty-four! I'm *sure* she must have had several love affairs. I bet she was engaged to be married, and he was killed in the war. I certainly expect to be married before I'm *that* old! I'm going to have eight children and live in a great big house."

"I'm *never* going to get married," said Nell. "I don't like boys. I don't care if I'm never invited to a ball game. I am going to be like Florence Nightingale and do something worthwhile in life."

"And don't you think it's worthwhile to get married and have lots of children?"

"Well, maybe, but I just don't want to."

"I hope you won't be like that awful Miss Miller, 'whose hair droops round her pallid cheeks like seaweed on a clam.'" They all laughed loudly.

"You wait and see. You'll change your tune when you start having dates and fun with boys."

"And what do you call 'fun'? Having a boy hold your hand and kiss you? My mother said it was wicked to allow a boy even to touch you. She told me about Edna who had to leave school because she let a boy touch her."

"And what do you call 'fun'? Having a boy hold your hand and kiss you? My mother said it was wicked to allow a boy even to touch you. She told me about Edna who had to leave school because she let a boy touch her."

"What about Edna? I knew she had to leave school; but what was it all about?"

"Why, didn't you know she was going to have a baby?"

In utter amazement, both girls almost shrieked, "NO!"

"Tell us about it. I didn't know you *could* have a baby if you weren't married," said Jane. "What an awful thing! I knew that everything was 'hush, hush' about Edna; but I never dreamed such a thing could happen at high school. Rosemary ran off and got married. But Edna! She seemed so nice! I can't believe it; I can't understand it, either."

"Well, she just let a boy kiss her, and that is what happened. My mother told me so."

"I just don't believe it," added Jane. "I'm going to ask Lady when I get to camp. She knows everything, and she knows Edna. She'll tell us all about it."

"Why don't you ask your mother to tell you?"

"Never! She would think I was awful even to think such thoughts. But I know one thing. Not every girl that holds hands with a boy and kisses him has a baby. Look at all the girls at school who are doing it all of the time! You just *have* to be married first. I don't care what anybody says. I bet Edna ran off and got married, and nobody knew it."

"Did you see that book that one of the senior high school girls had? She answered an advertisement that said that if you wanted to know all about marriage to send in a dollar and they would mail you a book in a plain envelope, so that no one would know what was in it. I just got a glimpse of it; but it was filled with all kinds of pictures. One of the teachers found it;

and was she mad! She took it away and said we had no business reading such things."

"I think we *ought* to have books like that," said Helen.

"The teacher must have read the book, for I heard her talking to another teacher at recess, and she said that next year we were going to have a course on getting ready for marriage; that even at our age we ought to begin to think about it."

Mrs. Brown in the next room had heard the conversation that had gone on during the toasting of marshmallows. She was dumbfounded. She had not thought for one moment that "those children" could be talking like that. In fact, she was horrified! But it had brought her to her senses, and she determined that something would have to be done about it. She felt relieved when Jane said,

"Give me one more marshmallow. The fire is going out and I must be going home. I still have a lot of things to do before I am ready for camp. Oh boy! Won't it be fun." The girls stretched as they got up, a bit stiff from sitting so long. Mrs. Brown then came into the room, considerably wiser than when she went out.

"Well, girls, are you ready? Jump in the car and I'll take you home."

Chapter 2

OFF TO CAMP

"Now, let's go over your list carefully to make sure nothing is omitted," said Jane's mother. "Don't forget that you won't have too much room for your things when you get to camp. You're allowed an army locker at the foot of your bunk bed, and then there is a small closet for each girl. Don't you remember you had to send home about half of your clothes last year because you had no room for them? Well, I'll read out what you have on your list, and you check: sheets, towels, soap, one heavy blanket, bathing suit."

"Yes, and just look at my bathing suit." Jane snatched it up and waved it in her mother's face. That had been the subject of many heartbreaking discussions; but Mrs. Clark had thought it had been settled, once and for all, that her last-year's bathing suit was good enough for another season. But no, once more she had to hear it all over again.

"Just look at this suit! You know blue is not my color. And the style of it belongs to the middle ages. They're just not wearing bathing suits this year with straps over the shoulders. You

know everyone is going to laugh at me when I put it on. I just wish the moths had eaten it all up! I never have liked it."

"Well, dear, you are the one that picked it out last year."

"I don't care. You made me buy it."

"You thought it was pretty *then*, for you told me so."

"*Then* it is not *now*. It is hideous, just hideous. But I suppose I'll have to take it," and she flung it into her trunk.

Her mother's heart sank into her shoes. She had hoped Jane's last day before leaving for camp would be so happy, thinking of the fun she would have and getting ready for it.

Just then, there was a banging at the door, and what looked like an army of girls burst into the room.

"Jane, Jane, the bus is going to be here an hour earlier than we thought! Why, aren't you packed yet? I was ready days ago. Hurry up, we'll help."

In a flash the locker was closed, the tennis racket put on top of it, and the accordion on top of that. The mother was ignored as they flew out the door and down the street to rush into somebody else's house. It looked as if every girl in town were going to camp. They passed Mary Ann on the corner surrounded by a group of boys. Some of the girls tried to josh her a bit, but she showed them that she felt very superior. The girls in the know laughed to themselves as they anticipated what was going to happen to her when Lady once gave one of her talks.

Honk! Honk! The camp bus swung round the corner and the girls all scampered, each to her own house, to stand ready by her belongings on the street so that no time would be lost in gathering everyone up. The mothers were trying to give last-

minute words of advice to deaf ears, but when the bus stopped for each girl, her mother did generally get a big hug with a, "Write me, Mom. Goodbye."

The bus was filled, and the girls shouted and yelled at everyone they saw as it rolled down the street and out of town. About half of the girls had been to camp the year before, but the other half were having this experience for the first time. If the truth were told, many of them were just a little frightened as they faced what to them was the unknown. Oh yes, they had heard a lot about everything, so as to know what to expect; and they had all thought that they wanted to go to camp, but somehow waving goodbye to their mothers gave their hearts a tug they had not expected.

But soon the old timers were singing the camp songs, and the new girls found themselves joining in. There were two counselors on the bus, Kay and Fay. They were so nice, seniors at college. The old camp girls were crazy about them and knew their personal lives from A to Z, knew all about their love affairs. And Kay this year was wearing a diamond! It was going to be thrilling to hear all about him and when they were going to be married, what her wedding dress was going to look like, and all the parties she would be going to. And my, all the presents she would get! What fun to get married! This is what most of them were thinking.

Kay and Fay were joining in the singing; but they also kept their eyes opened and watched each girl carefully. Kay noticed one little girl sitting by the window. She was younger than the rest. She was looking out the window and did not join in with

the singing. Kay quietly got up out of her seat and went over to Bessie, asked the girl next to her to change seats, and slipped in and sat down. Kay did not know her, for she was a new girl.

"My, doesn't the country look beautiful," said Kay.

Bessie, without looking up, said, "Yes."

"And have you ever seen Lake Laughing Water?"

"No."

"And is this the first time you have ever been away from home?"

"Yes."

Still the girl looked out of the window. She evidently was not anticipating much fun in going to camp. It was up to Kay to win her and to see that she had a good time. But something was evidently radically wrong. They both sat silent for a little while, then Kay began again:

"Have you any brothers or sisters?"

"Yes, a little brother."

"How old is he?"

"Six."

"Any more?"

Then Bessie's eyes filled up. She could hold in no longer.

"My mother is going to have a baby, and that's why they've sent me off to camp. They don't want me to be there when she dies."

"Dies! Why, she is not going to die!"

"Well, you know Mrs. Jones died when *she* had a baby."

"Oh, but she did not die because she had a baby. She had pneumonia at the time the baby was born. Why, to have a baby is nothing to be afraid of."

"Then why did they send me away?"

"Your mother wanted you to have a good time this summer, to get fat and rosy, and to learn how to swim and play tennis. For don't you know, you are going to help with the baby when you get back home. There is so much you can do. You will be giving the baby his bath. They are so cunning, too tiny at first to do much kicking; but when they are a few months old, they will splash you all over."

Bessie's face brightened for the first time.

"This baby of yours is going to think you are the most wonderful mother's helper in the world. All the girls at school will envy you and want to come home from school to see him. You can roll the carriage while mother takes a nap or does the ironing. My, my, you will have to have bushels of fun at camp, eat big meals and get strong, to do all of those things."

"And you really don't think my mother is going to die?"

"Why, of course not. To have a baby is the most natural thing in the world. That is one reason why girls like myself want to get married and have a baby, and I certainly hope that I will. Do you think I would, if I thought I was going to die? When does your mother expect the baby?"

"I don't know; she didn't tell me. All I know is the cleaning woman said, 'Your mother is sure going to have a big baby. I know she'll have a hard time. I never saw anyone so large in all my days.' It scares me every time I think of it."

"Look here, when you get to camp, Lady is going to tell you everything that you want to know. She'll tell us how babies are born and that there is nothing to be afraid of. Dr. Marilyn Johnson, whom you'll just love, comes to camp several times, and the

girls sit around the campfire while they ask her questions. She tells us how our bodies work and how we are different from boys and why. She says that girls in high school can begin to think about how to live so that they too can be mothers that their children will be proud of, just as you are proud of your mother.

"Oh, there's the lake. We were so busy talking I had forgotten to look out of the window and notice where we are. In just a few minutes you'll see the cabins. Now remember, I'm going to be in camp all of the time; so if there's anything that bothers you, or anything you want to know, you come right to me. I must be getting back to my seat and pull down my barracks bag."

Bessie, too, started to bustle around with an entirely different expression on her face from the one she had a little while ago. She was going to have fun at camp, so that she could help with that baby when she got back. Wouldn't mother be surprised when she saw what she could do!

Oh, there was so much excitement!

"Look! Look!" called out Jane. "Look, there's the new gym and dining hall. I did not expect it to be as big as all that. Now we can have games when it rains and at night. And there is Lady waiting for us! Why won't the driver open the door and let us get out? And old Joe is there, too. Look at him! He's beaming from ear to ear! I bet he's glad camp has opened and we have come. Mother thought my locker was too heavy, but you just watch. Joe will throw it on the truck as if it were a feather pillow."

Finally the door of the bus did open and out they all piled, almost on top of each other. Such hugging and kissing and crying

you never saw in all your life; but the funny thing was that the girls who were crying were the happiest. Those who did not quite know whether they were going to like it or not were just as solemn as owls, but they certainly shed no tears.

An earlier bus had come in from another town.

"Hello there, Fatty! But we can't call you 'Fatty' anymore. What have you done to yourself? You look six feet tall. 'Shorty' will have to be your name."

Before "Shorty" had time to turn around, someone from the rear had put her hand over her eyes.

"Guess who!" she called excitedly.

"I can't guess," and she jerked her hands down. Then more hugging.

"Oh, Jane, where are you going to be? In what cabin? Do you know your counselor? Let's try to get together again this year."

But the girls all knew that they could plan nothing. Everything that Lady said went. And they knew she was fair.

It was all so wonderful to be in camp again.

Chapter 3

THE FIRST CAMPFIRE

"There goes the bugle," the girls shouted. They all knew what that meant. They were starving, positively starving. And oh, everything tasted so good, even the much despised carrots; and somehow they drank all their glasses of milk. There was no urging. They took it for granted that it was the thing to do to eat what was set before them.

After lunch, the rest period. Would they have a rest period the first day of camp? Yes; for lunch was no sooner over than Lady rose and said:

"Each girl has already been assigned to her cabin and to her bunk. You have had a tiring trip. Many of you were up late last night packing. I shall expect quiet for one hour. No, you won't all sleep, but try to. If you can't, you may read or write letters; but no talking with your neighbor. I know you have hundreds of things to say, but there will be time for all of that. You may stay in your cabin when rest period is over, and unpack and get everything ready for inspection. Then we shall have games in the new gym at four, and campfire tonight. Remember, you

old girls have each been assigned a 'sister' to look after. Think up all the nice things that you can do for her to make her feel at home. You know how you felt when *you* first came to camp. Some girls did not like the cabins they were assigned. Some did not like the girls they were put with. Others wanted the same counselor that they had last year. While others were happy with anything and everything." And so the day passed, and evening came.

It was a perfect night, just ordered for the opening of camp. Even the moon was full; and the camp, with the shadows of the pine trees and the rippling of the lake, was like fairyland. The girls somehow caught the spirit of beauty and were all in the mood when the campfire was lighted, and they sat on benches in a semicircle around it. Lady was dressed in white with a dark blue scarf around her neck, looking her best. The girls gazed and adored.

Fay stepped forward and said:

"Let's sing the camp song. You old campers all know it; and those who are here for the first time will be singing it before the fire dies out... That's good; let's sing it again."

Lady's face beamed with pride as she looked over her girls who had been put under her care. They had such eager faces, and were so trustful. Her heart was going pit-a-pat, more than any of the girls imagined. She was so anxious to say just the right thing, so that each girl would grow into womanhood in a wiser, better way than if she had never come to camp. She had a great responsibility. She had heard so much about the way the teen-agers were behaving, that she was determined that

no girl should leave camp without knowing the facts about life. So she was going to start in at the very first campfire to let them know her plans.

Lady rose and started to speak, but the girls all burst into song. "She's a jolly good fellow!" She lifted her hand and quieted them a little sooner than she usually did; she looked a little more serious, too. Some were beginning to wonder if they were going to have as much fun this year at camp. But it was not long before Lady was laughing and telling all about the program of swimming, horseback riding and tennis, and what it meant to play the game fair and square. Still, there was an undercurrent of something, and she became a little more serious as she said:

"As a rule, our first campfire is spent in singing and telling experiences of what we've done this past winter. But so many of you are old-timers that I am going to start right in as if we had been here for a month. The summer is all too short for what we want to do this year. We are going to have just as much fun in every way, but added to that fun is going to be something very special. We are going to study the most interesting subject in all the world–ourselves. Each girl here is a book to study, and you are the ones to study the hardest to find out what is in those books. I am here to help you; the counselors are, too. Then we are going to have an expert, Dr. Marilyn Johnson, come and talk to us. She is a doctor who has worked with girls a lot. She is a mother and she knows how girls feel and think, and what they would like to know about their bodies as well as their minds. We want to go home from

camp knowing ourselves, so that each of us can better live with herself and know how to grow into the kind of woman she wants to be.

"You want to be liked by the boys, and you want to learn about them, too; not to mention, how to act when you are with them. It isn't easy for the boys either. They don't know very much about themselves; they have to work hard to find out what makes them act as they do. And can't they act up–so smart, as if they owned the world and were created just to be admired! Did it ever occur to you that they sometimes act that way just to cover up how insecure they really feel?

"They think they are 'no count'; and they even think that the girls don't like them! Isn't it funny that it should be like that! But it's true, for all of that. There is hardly a teen-ager, boy or girl, that does not have that inferiority feeling. But instead of acting inferior and humble, they just show off and make fools of themselves. If boys can't get attention because they play on the football team or excel in class, they try to get into the limelight by making a nuisance of themselves. Anything to be noticed.

"And how else do boys act? Well, we'll have to admit that some are just as courteous as can be, stepping back for a girl to go into a room first, and even picking up a book that might fall. You would think that girls would do anything to get a date with boys like that, but the show-off type attracts so much attention that some girls just fall for it. *They* want to be noticed, too. You may hear older people say, "Oh, they are young. They'll grow out of it." Sometimes they do; sometimes they don't. We

all know men and women that no one wants to be with. They have never grown up. They are *still* show-offs.

"I think some of you girls are old enough to think things through. You have hard subjects like algebra, English and history; and you have to use your brains to pass those courses. So why not study this most thrilling of all subjects, yourselves, and how you grow physically, mentally and emotionally? Maybe we can find out what it is that keeps some folks from becoming mature men and women. When you grow up, you want to take your places in the world, fully equipped in every way.

"How many of you have ever watched a little baby? (All hands went up.) What is it that the baby is most interested in? I mean a very tiny one. Mother? Yes, of course; but even before he cares much about his mother? Why does he cry? Yes, he is hungry. He doesn't much care who feeds him, just so he gets filled up with milk. And then he is so contented he just goes fast asleep.

"A little later he plays with his toes, sucks his fists. He takes pleasure in his own body; but before very long there is somebody else that comes into the picture. You have already guessed it: his mother. Then his father, his brothers and sisters, and others that may come into the home.

"Or, were this baby a girl, later on when she goes to school, she likes to play with girls her own age. She does not care much for the boys, I can assure you. They only tease.

"But a little later, when she gets to be your age, she begins to be interested in being with boys. She likes to have them around. She likes to talk with one and then another. It would bore her if

she thought she would have to go with one all of the time. She wants to look pretty, and she thinks about clothes a lot.

"Then, when she is a little older, she wants to go with one boy and only one. She does not enjoy being with the others. Then it is that young men and young women become engaged, marry and have children of their very own. Some are happily married; but we all know those who are not. Every single one that gets married wants to make a go of her marriage. So why doesn't she?

"There are many answers of course. But there is one big reason for a great deal of unhappiness; and that is that either the man or the woman has never really grown up. Perhaps neither has fully passed through all of the stages I have just told you about. To be sure, he doesn't remain a baby all of his life and play with his toes (a laugh from the girls). But I dare say that every one of you girls knows a boy that loves himself more than anything else in the world. He is proud of his muscles. He will look at himself in the mirror every chance he gets. He wants everyone else, especially girls, to look at him, too.

"Now, every boy and girl should take great pride in the way he or she looks; but if this boy that we have been talking about, or any other boy or man, keeps on just loving himself and thinking only of himself, he is not going to love the girl he marries as he should. He is what we call a poor marriage risk. He has never grown up past that stage of self-love.

"I have taken a boy as an example. But you girls have heard how some temperamental movie stars are–thinking only of themselves, how they look and how people go crazy over them.

"He is proud of his muscles. He will look at himself in the mirror every chance he gets. He wants everyone else, especially girls, to look at him, too."

No, most of this type are not happily married, either. But you don't have to be a movie star to love only yourself and keep that up till after you have married. Lots of ordinary folks fail just as badly.

"Why do I tell you all about this? Some people might say that you are not old enough to understand, but I believe you are.

Now is the time to study yourselves, at your very age, while you are growing up. If you know about life, it is so much easier to *keep from* making mistakes than it is to *undo* mistakes that you might make a little later because you did not know.

"I realize that I have given you a lot to think about; but you will be so busy swimming and hiking and horseback riding that you won't have time to think too much. That is the best way to grow up after all, happy in work and play and having just loads of fun.

"And now our evening song; and when taps comes, drop off to sleep and dream of tomorrow."

The girls had remained almost motionless for Lady's talk. Most of it was new to them, but they liked it. They liked to think of growing up and knowing how to do it right. They all wanted to ask Lady questions, but they knew that would come later.

The stars were shining, the moon was high in the sky, and the shadows were still dancing, when the last of the girls dropped off to sleep.

Chapter 4

WE WANT TO KNOW MORE

Lady was busily going over her accounts; she had gotten behind in her book work, and she simply had to shut herself up in her room and get that out of the way before the afternoon swimming meet. Feeling was running high as to which tribe would win, and she must be on hand in case any bitterness should break out. She did not enjoy those accounts. She much preferred to be with the girls. While she was adding up a column of figures, there was a knock at her door. She almost welcomed the interruption, but she did not expect what she saw. There stood a group of very serious looking campers with a look of anticipation on their faces which seemed to say, "You can answer all of our questions; and we really want to know." What faith the teen-ager has in us adults; if only we *did* know the answers!

"Well, girls, what can I do for you this time?" said Lady with a smile, as if time were no consideration to her at all.

Jane was the spokesman.

"We just wanted to talk to you. We want to know more about what you said to us last night at campfire. We don't understand some of the things that you told us."

Lady's office was well equipped for just such an intrusion. She had had girls knock at her door at other times, and they always came first, before any other business. Some sat on the big lounge, others on stools, while a few saw on chairs. They grouped themselves around her desk.

Lady began:

"I suppose I did try to tell you too much in one evening; but I just wanted to get the ball rolling, to make you girls think. We want to have plenty of time at the very beginning of camp to discuss all the angles of this important business of growing up. I am so glad that you have come to me so soon, and that you do have questions. We will try to answer them together; for I am sure some of you know the answers better than I. When I was your age, life was very different from what it is today, and so it is not always easy for me to put myself in your place. You will have to help me out–help me to see what your problems are. Well, who's first?"

Now Helen was the spokesman.

"I think I understand pretty well what you said about admiring ourselves and thinking that we are so wonderful–that clothes are the most important thing in the world, and the way we look. I know that is just about all I think about. I do want the boys to think I'm pretty."

"Now let me tell you something, Helen. I, too, hope the boys will think you are pretty. I hope you will always want to be well

dressed, and never look like a sloppy Joe when you are at a formal reception; that is a most important thing in a girl's life. But when you're older and get married, if you still keep on thinking that your dress and the shade of lipstick are the biggest things in your life, that to have a baby might spoil your figure, then you have not grown up emotionally. We could all name some women who are just like that; and I'm afraid they don't make their husbands very happy. They have kept on loving themselves just a little too long. I wonder if you have my point. It's most important.

"Every one of these stages we pass through has its good traits that we want to keep. But when you have no other interests, and hold on to these too long, then it is that you cannot be the woman that you want to be–and that your husband will expect you to be."

"But, Lady, you spoke about the baby loving her mother. Surely you never outgrow that? But to tell you the truth, I almost hate my mother at times right now. I could kick myself every time I do, but still I do. She is so unreasonable, looks upon me as a little girl, and acts as if I had no brains in my head. And she tells me what *she* did when *she* was a little girl. What do I care what she did then? She lived in the age of the dodo. Anyhow, I'm not a little girl."

Some of the other girls looked almost shocked at this outburst; though if they had spoken truthfully, they all had felt the same way at times. Strange as it may seem, it did not bother Lady in the least. She smiled.

"I'm so glad that Helen has spoken out as she has, for she has saved me the trouble of saying the same thing, only in a very

indefinite way. Each one of you girls (if you are normal–and I am very sure that you are!) is going to rebel against your mother at some time or other. But that does not mean that you are going to run away from home and be on your own, nor does it mean that you do not love her. It does mean that you have to begin to adjust and be a very different kind of a girl in the same environment.

"You can't change your mother, much as you wish you could at times. You can't throw your brothers and sisters out on the street. You have to live with the same furniture, which you think is too old-fashioned for words. How can you do it? Well, the answer is not easy. But you are on the right road when you begin now to think about all of this and to learn to know yourself, what makes you act as you do and why you have these strange thoughts.

"You don't have to be told (for you know it already) that you belong to that much-talked-of group, the teen-agers, that gives not only your mother a headache at times, but also your teacher, and anyone else that has anything to do with you. And, oh, how much they all want to help you! They make mistakes, of course. They say and do the wrong thing; but they are really interested in you and want you to be happy.

"But let's get back to your mother and what we were talking about last night. Even if you don't like your mother at times, you still love her. And I want you to believe me when I say it is nothing to worry about if you rebel a bit at the dress you are told to wear. You are not a little girl anymore. You ought to be choosing your own clothes. You ought to be fixing up your

room in a different way from when you were a child. Talk this over with your mother sometimes, when she is in a good mood and you're feeling good, too. It will amaze you the way she will swing in and help instead of hindering. But when you get mad, and then she gets mad and flares back, what have you accomplished? Absolutely nothing.

"About this mother-love stage of development, there is more to that than meets the eye. If when you are eighteen or twenty you would rather be with your mother than go out with a boy, then you are lingering too long in that little girl mother-love stage. It is far more natural for you then to want to be with the boys than to want to go places with just your parents. Always, always you will love your mother, more so as the years go by. But if, when the time comes that you want to get married, you feel you must live with your mother or have her come live with you, or at least be near enough so she can tell you what to do, then watch out! There is a danger signal ahead for an unhappy marriage.

"The same thing is true of the boy. Even more so. Beware of the boy whose mother is his only real interest, or whose mother hovers over him and wants to be the one to whom he constantly turns. Better leave him alone; for he is a big marriage risk. We all admire the boy who is thoughtful of his mother, for it is absolutely true that he will be thoughtful of his wife. That is a very different thing from what we call a 'mother fixation.'"

"Oh," sighed Helen, "I feel better now. I thought I was the only one who got out of patience with her mother, for other mothers always seem to know what to do better than mine; but as I think things over, I would not want to exchange her. I'm

"Beware of the boy whose mother is his only real interest, or whose mother hovers over him and wants to be the one to whom he constantly turns. Better leave him alone, for he is a big marriage risk."

going to write her tonight and tell her how much I love her, for I said so many mean things before I left for camp. I'm going to tell her how much better I'm going to be when I get back."

"Better keep that as a surprise," said Lady with a smile. "The battle is not won yet: But it will be."

The girls were reluctant to leave, but it was time for swimming, so Lady pushed them out of the door. "More another day."

When they were outside, they saw the girls all running to the lake. There was great excitement over who would be the winner. Helen and Jane held back a bit as they walked along together.

"I don't know whether I ought to go in swimming today or not. This is my first day. Mother says I shouldn't take a bath even at that time of the month. I feel perfectly well, though," said Jane.

"I know one thing. I wouldn't dare to go swimming; for I have cramps if I do the slightest thing the first day. I just have to take a day off. Look at Edith. She pays no more attention to it than if it did not exist. I really do envy her. I wish that Dr. Johnson would hurry up and come to camp and talk to us. Then we could ask her all about this, for she would really know. I think camp is wonderful this year. I never dreamed we were going to have all these interesting talks about things I have wondered about for so long."

Lady was hard at work again over her books when the phone rang. It was Dr. Johnson. The girls heard her say (for the door was open), "Yes, indeed, tomorrow night will be fine, the sooner the better. We'll be looking for you." Lady was delighted that she could come so soon after the opening of camp. She was very anxious for the girls to have time to think things over. It takes time to grow. It takes time to learn how; and it takes time to have long thoughts, and dreams of the future, when wedding bells will ring.

Chapter 5

DR. MARILYN JOHNSON SPEAKS

"Yes, girls, Dr. Johnson is coming tonight. She is going to talk in the gym at seven. Just wear blue shorts as usual. It will be very informal. But I want every girl to be there. Pass the word around, and put a notice on the bulletin board."

Even the old girls did not know quite what it was all about. This was something new at camp, to study about themselves. They did not have to be urged to go to the gym. They were there, and ahead of time. They sat on the floor in groups, not in a formal circle as they sometimes did.

Lady and Dr. Johnson each had a chair, and Lady had placed a little stand beside Dr. Johnson's, thinking she might be using notes. But no indeed! She stood right up and started to speak, just as if she were talking to each girl and to her alone. Everybody loved her at once.

She began by telling a lot of stories. The girls laughed heartily and almost began to think she had forgotten she was

a doctor. But before long she became quite serious, and so did they. This is what she said:

"I'm going to talk to you this evening exactly the way I talk to my medical students. I'm going to tell you just what I tell them, the whole story of how your body works, at your age. I'm going to use scientific terms, too. If you understand what they mean (and I'll explain each one as we go along), it is so much more definite and satisfactory than using baby words or more familiar language.

"In the science books you girls are spoken of as "adolescents." That means "becoming adult." You prefer to think of yourselves as "teen-agers." But whatever you call yourselves, you've probably noticed that certain changes are taking place inside you, though probably you haven't stopped to think too much about it. You don't understand what they are or what they mean, though you do feel them happening. See if you don't know what I mean.

"You used to pay little or no attention to boys, except to think them nuisances when you had to play games with them, or to hate them when they got big enough to tease you while you wanted to play with the other little girls. But a change has come over you lately. Not over all of you, but most of you girls who are here listening to me tonight have changed the way you look at boys and think about them.

"They're probably even more noisy and bothersome than they used to be. At least, older folks think they are. But to you, they have become interesting, and you want them to find you interesting, too. You don't mind their being clumsy,

and boisterous and not too polite. You are beginning to think of them as romantic, maybe a little bit mysterious even, certainly desirable to have around, even though you are not always quite certain how to act so as to make them *want* to come around. You may even actually begin to dream about them, and not only when you're asleep, but sometimes when you are wide awake, too, apparently! (Here the girls laughed, rather nervously.)

"Then, too, you are beginning to think about what is going to happen to you when you get older. Of course, every one of you expects to get married, even those few who insist that they don't; and equally, of course, you expect to have children. You don't know just who your husband is going to be–that you'll decide on later–but somehow or other, whenever you dream about your hero, he vaguely resembles some one of the boys you know or have been hoping to meet. You don't know how or when all this is going to happen. You only know that it *is* going to, some time in the future.

"Along with these changes in the way you *feel*, you and your girl friends are beginning to notice a change in the way you *look*. Up to now, you've simply been growing bigger and taller and heavier. But of late, you've begun to notice slight but quite definite changes in your figure. Some of you girls are fatter, some not so fat; but it's not only that. Your hips are a little broader; your legs are getting longer; your breasts, that used to be flat on your chests, are rounding out. In other words, you are beginning to have some curves, instead of being all angles, the way you were as long as you were little

Up to now, you've simply been growing bigger and taller and heavier. But of late, you've begun to notice slight but quite definite changes in your figure. Some of you girls are fatter, some not so fat; but it's not only that. Your hips are a little broader; your legs are getting longer; your breasts, that used to be flat on your chests, are rounding out.

girls. You have noticed, too, a little growth of hair beginning under your armpits and in your groins. What do you suppose it is that causes all these strange changes to happen in your bodies and in your minds, too?

"Well, there are two little glands in the body of every girl or woman, one on each side. They are called ovaries because their job is to manufacture and turn out a tiny egg every month. The Latin word for egg is *ovum*. Nothing mysterious about that, is there?

"But they also manufacture something whose action *is* mysterious and hard to understand. It's called estrogen; and it has the magic power of turning a girl into a woman! It not only makes you *look* like a woman, instead of like a little girl; it makes you *feel* and *think* like one, too, and begin to dream about growing up, and falling in love, and marrying, and having children. And along with all these new ideas go a lot of vague, rosy-tinted dreams about boys, and later on about one special boy. This is what we call romance.

"Later on we'll talk about these changes in your thoughts and feelings, and what they do to you, and how they can help you if you understand how to manage them, and how they can harm you if you don't. But tonight I want to stick to the physical side and explain to you a little more about what happens in these two manufacturing plants, the ovaries.

"I told you a moment ago that every four weeks or so one of them sends out an ovum. This is a tiny microscopic speck, about $1/125$ of an inch long. Now where do you suppose it goes to?

"Well, it is wafted right into a tube called the Fallopian tube (after Fallopius, a 16th century physician) that takes it into the womb, or uterus, an organ about the size and shape of a pear, situated in the center of the body. Here it stays for a few days, and then is detached and thrown out of the body. Along with it

goes some of the lining of the uterus which had become thickened in order to receive and take care of it, as well as a certain amount of blood.

"When this happens, and it takes four days, more or less, for the discharge to be over and done with, we say that a girl is "having her monthly period." Some people still call it her "monthly sickness," for it used to be considered a time when a girl was expected to be sick, and to avoid all sorts of exercise, or even activity of any sort.

"But we are going to use the scientific term here as everywhere else, as I told you we should; so we'll say that she is menstruating. And as we're going to be accurate as well as scientific, we won't call it a "sickness," nor yet "the curse," as some girls foolishly term it.

"The age at which they begin having their monthly periods (what folks call "the beginning of puberty"), is very different in different girls. Probably most girls start between the ages of twelve and fourteen; but they may begin as young as ten or eleven, or even earlier. And some girls don't commence to menstruate until they are fifteen or sixteen years old.

"Some girls are, as we say, perfectly regular. They flow for four days, every twenty-eight days, right from the start. Others, while they eventually become quite regular, may skip a month or two at the beginning. The duration of the flow, too, varies from one day to several; and it may be very scanty, or quite profuse. These variations should not be looked upon as indicating that anything is wrong. Such wide variations are perfectly possible within the limits of the normal.

"What is *not* all right, and is certainly not to be neglected, is this business of painful menstruation that troubles so many girls. To be sure, it is not at all unusual for a girl to have a moderate amount of discomfort, and even a little bit of pain, especially at the starting up of the flow each month. The uterus is sometimes tipped at an angle with the vagina, into which the flow is emptied; and that makes it a little difficult for the discharge to escape. But any pain or discomfort is sufficient to make it the business of any mother to take her daughter to her family physician. He can usually detect the little irregularity that is the cause of the discomfort and correct it without much difficulty.

"I imagine that most of you girls probably had some hazy idea of what menstruation was like before it started. But many of you dreaded it, without any very definite knowledge as to what it was all about. Even if your mothers had told you all they knew about it, as more and more mothers are learning the advisability of doing, you may have dreaded it. Perhaps you feared that it might mean severe pain, or the loss of a dangerous amount of blood, or something else equally frightening–but, as I can now assure you, equally untrue!

"On the other hand, a number of you, instead of dreading the starting of your monthly periods, have looked forward eagerly to this as a sign that you are growing up. And indeed it is–one of the first signs that you are leaving childhood and entering girlhood. You want, of course, to enjoy being what you are, as each day comes along; but life would be dull indeed if we could not anticipate the future with keen pleasure.

"Girls sometimes worry if they 'skip a period'; and think they ought to do something, like taking a hot bath, or taking some medicine, to 'bring it on.' There are several things that may cause such a failure of a period to come at the expected time. We'll talk about that at our next get-together.

"In the meantime you may wonder, as you have probably often wondered in the past, what all this rather bothersome business, that is sometimes embarrassing and often decidedly inconvenient, is designed for. You may be sure that it serves a useful purpose. Nature seldom or never does things without good and sufficient reason. But it's too late to go into that big subject tonight. Next time I meet with you, we'll take that up and discuss some of the interesting things you'll want to know about it. But for now, goodnight."

Chapter 6

THE MYSTERIES OF LIFE ARE EXPLAINED

To have Dr. Marilyn Johnson talk to the girls so frankly and clearly was an experiment at camp; and if the truth were told, Lady was a little anxious as to how it would be received. But her fears were all unnecessary. The girls chatted about Dr. Johnson's talk with great interest, as they should have done; but not once did she hear a vulgar remark or a giggle as if knowledge were funny. They were eager to be told more. Lady thought it wise while their thoughts were on the lecture to have another talk follow immediately; and so it was arranged for Dr. Johnson to come the next night. There was no need of any introduction, so she began:

"You will remember my telling you about the journey taken by the ovum that one or other of the ovaries produces every month or so. I told you that it travels along the Fallopian tube till it enters the uterus. It clings to the inner wall of the uterus for a few days, and then is washed out along with the rest of the menstrual discharge.

"But sometimes the ovum is *not* discharged. No menstrual flow takes place; and the ovum continues to cling to the wall of the uterus. This is because something very special has happened to it, which makes it a very important bit of matter, indeed. But before I tell you what that something special is, I must explain to you something else, about which you have undoubtedly wondered. That is, just how boys differ from girls.

"I don't mean in their looks, or their actions, or their clothes, or the part they play in life. I mean about the workings of their bodies and how they compare with some of the things I told you last time about *your* bodies. One of the amazing things about us, men and women, is that, although we are so different in almost every way, there are a number of things about us that are astonishingly similar. You'll see what I mean by this confusing statement in just a minute, for I'm going to tell you in detail some of the similarities and some of the differences.

"For example: The girl has two almond-sized glands, the ovaries, that manufacture the female elements, the ova. The boy has two similar-sized glands, the testicles, that manufacture the male elements, the spermatozoa, or sperms. But the ovaries are situated *in*side the girl's body, while the testicles are carried in a pouch called the scrotum, *out*side the boy's.

"Another difference is one for which it is hard to see any reason. The two ovaries, between them, produce but one ovum a month, whereas the testicles are producing hundreds of millions of sperms and producing them constantly.

"Again, the ovaries pour out a secretion, estrogen, that changes a girl into a woman. The testicles pour out a secre-

tion, testosterone, that changes a boy into a man. Each of them, in addition to changing a child into an adolescent and then into an adult, makes one sex interested in being with the other and in coming into close contact with the other; and each of them makes both the young man and the young woman want to have children. But there is a difference here too, as well as a similarity. For while the desire to have children and the thought of them (even though of course she does not want them at once) appears fairly early in the adolescent girl, it appears much later in the adult man. This difference has quite a different effect when the question of marrying comes into the picture.

"Now ever since I mentioned that sometimes something very special happens to one of these ova in the course of its journey from the ovary to the uterus so that it doesn't have to be thrown out at a period; some of you girls have been wondering just what that something might be. Some of you older ones have guessed it already, I imagine. Now I'm going to tell you what it is.

"When a man and a woman love each other enough to forsake all others and cleave (that is, cling) to each other as long as they both shall live, they marry. They have made love to each other during their courtship and engagement. But after they have become man and wife, a further experience, which is called intercourse, awaits them.

"If they desire it, their lovemaking may sometimes have a wonderful result. One of the millions of sperms I told you about joins the ovum that is traveling toward the uterus. When these

"When a man and a woman love each other enough to forsake all others and cleave (that is, cling) to each other as long as they both shall live, they marry. They have made love to each other during their courtship and engagement. But after they have become man and wife, a further experience, which is called intercourse, awaits them."

two tiny, life-bearing particles, a male sperm and a female ovum, unite, we say that the ovum has been fertilized. Another way of expressing it is to say that the wife has become pregnant.

"The result is the very first stage in the life of a new human being with all the possibilities of attainment that lie before a completely separate personality. In nine months, or thereabouts, this tiny mite will have grown large enough to exist separately from its mother. Then, it will be expelled from the uterus, where it has been so carefully nourished and kept warm, right close up under its mother's heart.

"So far I've been telling you a great truth. But to be absolutely fair and square with you, I'll have to confess that what I've told you is in reality only half the truth, the beautiful half of a truth that has a very unhappy, sordid, dreadful side. I've told you that this business of creating a new life is the result of the act of a man and a woman who love each other well enough to become man and wife for life. The ceremony that blesses their union is a beautiful piece of consecration; but it in itself does not have anything to do with creating the new life. It is intercourse alone that makes that possible.

"Now the other half of this wonderful truth is that it sometimes happens that two people who do not love each other at all, or who love each other without having any right to have the experience we have been talking about that creates a new life because they are not married. They try to have it without any regard to whether it is right or wrong. What they are after is the physical sensation and thrill that they expect to get out of the experience; and the last thing they want or expect is to create a new life as a result of it.

"In fact, they usually take what they have been told are precautions that will insure that this will *not* happen.

And sometimes these precautions are successful. But sometimes it happens that they are not. And then, a terrible thing takes place.

"The woman (often she is just a girl) becomes pregnant, and a baby, whom society brands as illegitimate, is born. Then, the unfortunate involuntary mother is flung out of her place in the world and faces all sorts of grave problems.

"Now since the plight of the unmarried mother is so tragic, and since the man is condemned so by his conscience and by society, people who commit this immoral act are usually very fearful lest pregnancy take place, in spite of the precautions they may have taken. And one of the earliest signs of pregnancy is skipping a period.

"For this reason, girls who have always been regular sometimes become terrified if they happen to go over time. They have never been told, as every girl should be told, that this is not necessarily a sign of pregnancy. It may be due to fatigue, anemia, traveling, or any of several other things.

"Girls who do not know what I have told you, that intercourse is the only way pregnancy can be started, sometimes become panic-stricken, especially if they have been indulging in heavy petting, with prolonged kissing. They will turn anywhere for something to stop the supposed pregnancy. To meet this situation, and make an evil profit from it, an almost unbelievable practice has grown up.

"Unprincipled doctors, and equally unprincipled women, offer to give medicines, or even to perform a criminal operation, to bring on an overdue period and break up the supposed

or actual pregnancy. Law and religion both consider this murder of the unborn child. And since it may kill the pregnant girl also, or make her an invalid for life, you can see how foolish it is for a girl who has skipped a period to do anything except go to her doctor and follow his advice. He can put her fears at rest. But now to get back to what we were talking about before we got off on this unpleasant but important subject.

"I hope sometime I may get a chance to tell you girls about how the tiny life grows steadily larger during the nine months until at last it becomes mature enough to live by itself, without the constant warmth and nourishment that have been in evidence during this whole time. Then one day, by some mysterious arrangement that no one has yet been able to explain, a signal comes to the bodies of the baby and his mother announcing that the time has come when they must separate. This act of separation is known as confinement, labor and delivery for the mother, and as birth for the baby.

"You girls may have overheard older women talking (when they believed that you were not within earshot) about the terrible times some woman had to undergo when her baby was born. As a result of this loose talk, some of you may have come to look forward with dread to the experience, in your own case.

"This is just too bad because it is so unnecessary for you to have been scared this way. Advances in the practice of medicine and new discoveries in the way of useful drugs have robbed childbirth of its terrors. Even the 'labor pains' you may have heard older women allude to are now better and more accurately known simply as 'contractions' by which the baby is

carried along on his way to the outside world. Expectant mothers are now taught how they can help themselves; and many who have had one or more babies even look forward with eager anticipation to going through the experience again.

"It used to be considered out of the question for any girl to be told anything about how babies were born, or how their bodies were formed so as to perform this very necessary function. Boys and girls were given the impression by their elders that it was almost wicked for them even to think about how boys differ from girls. And never, never should a girl have the faintest idea of what takes place in marriage so that a new life can be created.

"You girls of today are indeed fortunate. For lack of knowledge about the facts of life is no longer considered a sign of innocence. Instead, it is rightly known to be gross ignorance. Immorality is frowned upon today as it was in those days when girls did not know what the term meant. Now that you do, it is up to you girls to set up standards so that marriage will never be debased from the sacred relationship God intended it to be.

"You know now, if you did not know if before, that heavy petting and experimenting can so debase it. So upon you rests the responsibility of keeping motherhood in its rightful place, as the greatest experience a woman can have. It has been truly said that 'the race moves forward on the feet of little children.'

"Right now, here in camp, you are preparing yourselves physically and spiritually so that when you are the mothers of tomorrow, the world will be a better place to live in because of you. As you keep yourselves fine, you influence every boy that is your friend. Yours is this trust. I believe you will keep it."

Chapter 7

MARY ANN RUNS AWAY

There was a banging at Lady's door, not a mere knock. Before she could say, "Come in," the door was pushed open and Kay, out of breath, gasped, "Lady, is Mary Ann here?"

"No, why?"

"She went down to practice archery; and when her turn came, she was nowhere to be found. One of the girls discovered a note in her cabin signed 'John.' It said, 'Meet me under the oak tree at four, and we'll go for a ride.'"

Lady jumped up, startled.

"Who is this John? Do you know him?"

"Yes, I am very sure he is the one that drives the laundry truck. One of the girls saw Mary Ann talking to him the first day of camp."

"Do you know what oak tree he meant?"

"Yes, it is that great big tree down by the lake, near those dense woods."

"Take your car and swing around there. Swing around everywhere at once! But say nothing to the girls yet."

"But Lady, the girls already know everything. The news spread around camp like wildfire."

"No time to waste. Hurry!"

So Kay ran out of the room while Lady tried to compose herself and think. She had anticipated trouble with Mary Ann from the very first; but she had hoped to win her, and certainly did not expect anything to take place quite so soon.

Supper time came and went, and no Mary Ann. The girls whispered in groups in subdued voices. The camp songs somehow did not go over very well. No one was in the spirit. An awful thing had taken place, and the girls did not know what was going to happen; but if the truth were told, they were having the time of their lives with all of this excitement.

What went on behind closed doors with Lady and the counselors, no one knew. But they all went to bed, and there was no Mary Ann. She had not gone home, for Lady had phoned her mother. But about eleven o'clock that night, Mary Ann slipped into her cabin. She had thought she could get into her bunk unnoticed, but Fay, her counselor, was still wide awake.

"Why, Mary Ann, I am so glad to see you," she whispered, lest she wake the girls. "Did you have a good time?"

"No."

"Well, Lady told me that when you came in, she wanted you to go and sleep in her room tonight."

"I don't want to, and I'm not going to."

"Oh, you know how sweet Lady is. She will be so happy to have you safely back. She was a bit worried, for you know how interested she is in you."

Fay took Mary Ann gently by the arm and led her out of the cabin, while all the other girls slept soundly. Lady was not asleep. She was sitting up by her phone, trying to read. When Mary Ann walked in, she just threw her arms around her and kissed her, and Mary Ann cried. Lady patted her and loved her a bit, made a cup of hot chocolate for her and gave her some of the cookies she always kept on hand for various and sundry occasions. She chatted about camp and what she liked best to do, but both knew that all of this was killing time. So Lady did not mince matters but came right to the point.

"Now, dear, tell me all about it. What made you run off without permission? Where did you go? And what happened? Had you ever known John before you came to camp?"

"Well, I just got tired of being cooped up with all these girls. Some may think it's fun to go swimming and play tennis, but that's not what *I* call fun. I want excitement and romance and a good time."

"And did you have a good time?"

"To tell the truth, no. I wish I had never run off. I hope I shall never see John again as long as I live. I hate him!"

"Now tell me. Where did you go, and what did you do?"

"I met John under the oak tree, and he told me to hop in his car and we'd go for a ride, that he'd get me back in time for supper, and no one would ever know that I'd been away. It was a beautiful day for a drive; so why shouldn't I? We drove and

drove all over, and then he took me for supper at the Piggie-Wiggie House. After supper, he said that he thought it would be fun to dance a bit. It was a little rowdy, and I didn't like the looks of the girls there, nor the boys and men, either. I also thought of my mother, and camp, and what you all would be thinking if you could see me. But I had not danced in so long! It really was fun, in a way.

"About nine, I told John I thought it was about time to go back to camp, so that I could slip in and no one would see me. He said 'No, let's spend the night here. I'll get you back before anyone wakes up, and no one will know about a thing.' But I did not want to. I told him I *had* to get back; that you would be worried. I saw no sense in spending the night. He begged and begged me, but I ran out and jumped into the car. It was dark coming home, and I didn't enjoy it. He kept putting his arm around me and hugging me, and then would give me a kiss. I had never had a man really hug me like that before. And all at once he drew the car up to the side of the road and stopped. I said, 'What's the matter? Is there a puncture?' He did not say a word, just hugged and kissed me more and–"

"And what else?" said Lady, trying to act composed.

"And I began to get scared. I don't know exactly why, but I began to think about what Dr. Johnson had told us and I did not know what was going to happen next. I got so scared I jumped up and screamed at him, 'Take me back to camp! I want to go home!' This kind of brought him to his senses; and he sat back in the seat and stepped on the gas, and we started. I thought we would *never* get back to camp over that long road.

"He kept putting his arm around me and hugging me, and then would give me a kiss. I had never had a man really hug me like that before. And all at once he drew the car up to the side of the road and stopped. I said, 'What's the matter? Is there a puncture?'"

He did not talk to me much, just acted hateful and said that he was never going to take me out again."

Lady was still composed in her manner; but she was not satisfied with the whole story.

"Mary Ann, I want you to answer me one question very honestly. Did John try to take off any of your clothes?"

"Yes, he jerked at my dress. But I got mad and told him to stop."

"Are you absolutely sure?"

"Absolutely and positively! No, Lady, nothing more happened than I have told you. I have not kept one thing back. I am telling you the truth and nothing but the truth. I know I did wrong." Mary Ann started to cry again.

"Please don't tell my mother; and *please* don't send me away from camp. I'll never, never do anything like that again. You had better tell the girls what I did, so that they won't go riding with John."

"You need not worry. John will never enter camp again with his truck. But there are other Johns. Every girl must know what the consequences may be, if she gets into a car with a man she does not know. Girls cannot be protected every minute. They must know facts and protect themselves. It is late, almost one o'clock. Here, take a pair of my pajamas, and roll up on the cot. You can sleep in my room tonight. We'll talk about your plans tomorrow."

"But please tell me that I can stay on here. Please, *please*!"

"Now don't you worry about that now. You just drop off to sleep," and Lady leaned over and kissed her on the forehead.

"Oh, Lady, you don't know how glad I am to be here and not in that awful Piggie-Wiggie. That is an awful place. It really is."

"Now don't think of that any more; but dream about how you are going to win the tennis match tomorrow."

Mary Ann tossed a bit; but soon was sleeping so soundly that nothing could have disturbed her. And so Lady crept into her bed; but somehow she could not sleep quite so soundly. She knew the girls would have to be told more than Dr. Johnson had told them. Mere physiological facts were not enough. Mary

Ann's conduct had proved that. She used to think that if girls knew the facts of life, nothing else was necessary. But now she knew better. She really had known (though she hated to face it) that two girls had to leave high school because they were pregnant. And they certainly had taken the prescribed course in hygiene. She was determined to give her girls the whole truth from every possible angle, make them not only know, but think things through; and if possible, inspire them with an ideal, plus their knowledge. She kept thinking to herself, *knowledge is not enough*.

Lady was up a little earlier, if anything, than usual the next morning. She let Mary Ann sleep on. At breakfast she announced,

"I am glad to say that Mary Ann is safely back, and that everything is going to be all right. She did not get in till late, so I thought it best to let her sleep and get slept out. And, girls, I would appreciate it if you do not ask her too many questions. You all know that she ran off with John and took a drive in his car; and I can assure you that nothing really serious happened. Enough happened for me to want to have a real heart-to-heart talk about petting or necking and how girls your age should really act with a boy. Mary Ann did a very dangerous thing when she went off with a strange man in his car. She has learned her lesson; but I want you to learn yours without suffering what she suffered. She thought she was going to have such fun, but it was far from it. Let's sit around the open fire tonight and talk and ask questions, and learn to know ourselves just a little better. I'll see you at seven."

Chapter 8

WHAT'S THE HARM? PETTING

Never had the girls seen Lady so serious. They knew that Mary Ann had run away, but she had gotten back. So what of it? They had taken rides with boys themselves. There was no harm in that. To be sure, she ought not to have gone without permission, but that was not enough to have made Lady act as solemn as she had all day. The girls wanted to get it over with if she had anything awful to tell them. They heard at supper what they had expected to hear, that there would be a talk in the gym that night.

When they had assembled, there was no delay. She began: "Girls, I need not tell you what happened yesterday, for you all know it already; and Mary Ann has given me permission to use her as the subject of our discussion. She is right here with us, and I am sure she will agree with what I am about to say. Dr. Johnson has gone into great detail about what changes are now going on in your bodies and how you differ from boys. She told you that when a young man and a young woman marry, one of

the things they look forward to is having a baby of their very own. She told you how that baby was created, by the union of the male sperm and the female egg.

"I am afraid that Dr. Johnson did not make it clear that sometimes that very beautiful experience can be a most horrible one. Can you imagine anything worse than finding out that you were going to be a mother when you were not married and you had never wanted a baby at all? There is not a girl here who does not know that two girls had to leave school last year for that very reason. Everybody tried to hush it up, but everybody knew it.

"What happened? I knew one of the girls quite well, and she told me her story. She had been running around with one of the boys in town who did not have any too good a reputation. But he had a car, and she thought it didn't matter just to have a little excitement and fun. One night, they drove out to a roadside café for supper. They each took a little drink, not much. No, they did not get drunk. They danced and got excited, as a drink will make you; and before she knew it, she was in his arms out in the car. He was hugging her and kissing her, just as Mary Ann said happened to her.

"But Mary Ann had not had a drink. She came to her senses and stopped short and demanded to be taken back to camp. But this poor girl hardly knew what was happening to her. The boy would not let her go; and she did not want him to at the moment. But when all was over, she was most unhappy, and he drove her home.

"She tried not to think anything more about it, but one day she went to the doctor's because she had skipped two of her monthly periods, and she had always been regular before. The

doctor had the heartbreaking task of having to tell her and her mother that a baby was on the way. No, there was absolutely nothing else to do but to go through with the ordeal. It is positively against the law to take a life that has been started. And then, even if the doctor had been willing to commit a crime, it would have been a most serious operation, and might have cost the life of the girl. She just had to go away, always with this blot upon her reputation, and with the baby branded as illegitimate."

"Well, *I* think the *man* was to blame," one girl called out; "and I think he should have been put in jail! It isn't fair!"

"No. It is not fair, not at all. But you must know, and have it burned into your consciousness, that the girl is always the one to suffer most when, unmarried, she becomes a mother. It is something that I simply hate to think about–that such a wonderful experience for those who are married can be turned into such a nightmare for those who are not married. Fun! Was that girl having fun? You need not answer, for you know.

"But the happy thought is, that it never need happen. Everyone can wait till married, both boys and girls, men and women. There is one rule to remember: Avoid prolonged petting; for it can only lead to trouble."

"What do you mean, Lady?"

"I mean just this. Hugging and kissing (petting) can be carried on so long that neither the boy nor the girl seem to be able to stop. And this is where drinking is always harmful. It makes your emotions go fast. You loosen the brakes, and you lose control."

"Do you mean that you should never let a boy put his arm around you?"

"No, not at all. It is all right to see you young people go hand in hand. If a boy really cares for a girl, a goodnight kiss after a date or a handshake that shows a little feeling can hardly be termed going too far. But there is a very thin line drawn between what is going too far and what is not. Better err on the side of being considered too reserved, than of being too cheap with your kisses. And you do not have to act like a 'touch-me-not,' either.

"Every worthwhile boy will respect you for this. The girl is the one that sets the pace. If she does not care how much the boy fondles her, and if she doesn't care how far he goes, there is no telling to what limits he *will* go. Yes, I blame the girls many, many times for allowing liberties with the boys. This is a new age, I know, and the girls have a freedom they never had before. But it makes me boil when I see a girl abuse that freedom and encourage a boy to do what she knows he has no business to do."

Lady sounded almost angry. The girls knew that this was a pretty serious subject; and not one of them missed the point. As young as they were, they knew what she was talking about. She had the girls with her, too. They knew she was right; and they determined right then and there that they were going to have a happy marriage and not do anything beforehand to spoil it. They were going to help the boys to go straight, too.

The girls were all bursting with questions.

"Lady, do you think it is all right, when you are engaged to be married, to let a boy kiss you a lot?"

"That is a little different story. That goes into what we call courtship and marriage. You will take courses in that later. But I will say in answer to your question (and every question

deserves an answer), that when young men and women of college age or over are engaged to be married, it is quite all right for more affection to be shown; but never, never should that line be crossed that we have been talking about, even though they are soon to be married."

"Can you get a baby if you just let a man kiss you a very long time?"

"No, that is impossible. There is only one way that a baby can be started; and Dr. Johnson has told us all about that."

"Do you think the reason that my mother is all the time fussing about my hitch-hiking, and getting into a car with a man I don't know, is because she is afraid that something like this might happen?"

"Yes, Edith. I *know* that is the reason, the main reason. She wants to protect you. For again, I hate to say it, but more than once, a hitch-hiker has had just such an experience. And what is more, sometimes the nicest looking man will ask to take you home from school in his car. If you do not know him, it is wise for you to thank him and tell him that you are taking the bus."

"I want to ask a question about drinking. Do you think that one cocktail will hurt anyone? My mother and father take *their* cocktails."

"Again, Jane, I am not a very good one to ask; for when I am at a cocktail party, I always ask for ginger ale. No one cares whether I drink or not. Again, as with smoking, there is a big difference of opinion, and people whose opinion I highly prize do not have my convictions about it. But we all agree on one thing, without a dissenting vote. And that is, that for

teen-agers, any form of alcoholic drink is very, very harmful. You must know that your bodies have not matured, and your emotions are still easily upset. Why add a stimulant to make it harder to control them? For the next few years, you are going to have a hard enough time to hold back tempers and control yourselves in a hundred ways. And so, if anyone offers you a drink of *any* kind: Be on the safe side, and ask for a soda."

A hand went up. Lady nodded to Nell.

"I wish you would explain one more thing about petting. It *must* be lots of fun; or so many boys and girls would not do it."

"Ask Mary Ann if she thought it was fun, the night she ran off with John. She is shaking her head 'no.' Yes, there is a certain amount of physical pleasure in prolonged kissing and embracing, but there is not much pleasure when you stop short. Then you have a sort of contempt for yourself for having spent the evening that way.

"Do your thinking first. Plan something that is a really good time. There is much more fun if you go out in groups and have your boy and girl pleasures together at picnics and at the gym. Now is the time for you to meet a lot of boys and learn how to talk to all kinds. When you are older and reach what they call 'the mating age,' then you will prefer to be with only one boy. You'll like to talk with him about all kinds of things. You'll like to go to places of interest with him. Yes, you'll want to be alone with him, and you should. But right now, you are not at that age. You will have loads more fun by going in groups."

"Lady, when one of the girls at High left school last year to have a baby, I heard one of the older girls say that she was stupid,

that there was no need for her to have had that baby at all. She could have prevented it. Is that true?"

"Yes, there *are* things that can be done to prevent 'conception,' as it is called. But there is nothing that is 100% sure. And I would rather not go into that now, for all of it is absolutely unnecessary, if you girls keep yourselves pure, keep yourselves with high ideals. No, that is not being old-fashioned; it is the very latest style. Have as your motto 'It's Smart To Go Straight.' And don't you think a happy marriage is reward

"And don't you think a happy marriage is reward enough? To have a fine, upright man in love with you, who wants you for his wife and to be the mother of his children, is worth a hundred petting parties. Don't you think so?"

enough? To have a fine, upright man in love with you, who wants you for his wife and to be the mother of his children, is worth a hundred petting parties. Don't you think so? And that is just what you have to look forward to, if you keep true to the ideals we have talked about in camp. And the most wonderful thing about being your age is that you have not done things to regret; that you can face life with knowledge and confidence. You are so sweet and lovely now; you can stay that way.

"Some of you girls may feel that I keep saying the same thing over and over. Maybe I do in order to get it fully across. And so at the expense, perhaps, of saying it again, I want to put upon you more responsibility in your relationship with your boy friends. Maybe there should be an absolute equality between boys and girls, but there isn't, and you girls must face it. Boys are physically more impulsive. It is you. It is you that encourages them in heavy petting. You are the one that can keep not only yourself moral and straight but the boy straight also. And never forget, it is you that suffers the most, not the boy, when your petting goes too far. Maybe you will escape pregnancy by some good fortune. But you have endangered yourself just as much as if you had jumped in front of a rushing train in hopes that you could get across and not get hit. So look both ways before crossing the track.

"If any of you girls want to come to me privately and ask any more questions, you know I am always ready to help.

"Good night and happy dreams. And may your prince come riding by and take you off one of these days."

Chapter 9

THE GIRLS TRY TO UNDERSTAND THEIR MOTHERS

The days were just flying; camp was almost half over. Some of the girls would be leaving then, and a few new girls would be coming. It did not seem possible that time could have flown so fast. Lady began to realize (so eager had she been to have the girls understand themselves in regard to the growth of their bodies and all the changes that were taking place within them, and to know about boys in the same way) that she was almost neglecting one of the most important adjustments that any teenage girl has to make—her attitude toward her mother. That subject was fraught with more explosives than almost anything else. Somehow the girls got along pretty well with their fathers, at their age, but their mothers were a constant source of irritation. And so at supper, when the announcements were being made, Lady said:

"Tonight around the campfire we are going to have an open discussion. And what do you thing the subject will be? Our mothers! They won't be anywhere around, so we can just pick them to pieces all we want to. Be thinking about all the things your mothers do, that you wish they would *not* do; and all the things you wish they *would* do that they don't. It won't be so very long before you will be going home and there you will have many a problem to face. Can't you hear your mother say, 'Now, dear, *don't* put on that bright lipstick. You are too young. And besides, school is no place to be looking as if you were going to a party.'" The girls all laughed; for how true, all too true, were those words.

"We'll toast some marshmallows around the fire, too, and sing. Better put on your sweaters, for it is just a little cool."

The girls began to buzz at once with each other as to what they liked and didn't like in their mothers. It was just as well that their mothers did not hear them; for unless they had been most understanding, it would not have made them very happy. Most of them were trying so hard to be good mothers; and then to see how they were failing in the eyes of their daughters would have made them sad indeed. But had they realized that every mother was in the same fix with her own teenage daughter, it might have been a comfort. It just seems to be Nature's way in this growing up process. It is not easy for mother or daughter.

The campfire burned. The girls were all seated around it, and Lady began:

"First, I have a big surprise for you. I have just had a telephone message that Bessie has a little baby sister!"

There were "Ahs" and "Ohs."

"Let's give our camp yell for her; for she will be coming to camp, one of these days. Her father said that the baby was a little beauty, and her mother was so happy to have another girl. It is going to be hard now to keep Bessie in camp. She is going to want to go home and take care of that baby of hers. She can do so much to help her mother. It will be such fun to work with her."

"Well, I can tell you one thing. *I* don't think it's fun to have to look after my two-year-old brother when I want to go out and play," exclaimed Jane.

"All right," said Lady, "Jane has started the ball rolling. She starts out with the first point as to what we don't like in our mothers. She does not like to be called upon as a babysitter. Who next? Let's go right around, one after another, with just a sentence or two. All right, Helen."

"I don't like the way my mother tells me to fix my hair."

"Nor I," shouted another.

"I want to choose my own clothes, and my mother won't let me."

"I wish she wouldn't tell me that I am cold when I'm not and make me put on a warm dress that I nearly burn up in."

"Why does my mother have to tell me to turn off the radio and say that I shouldn't be listening to such stuff, just because she doesn't happen to like murder mysteries?"

"When I go to a party, she calls twelve o'clock late to come home. Other mothers aren't like that."

"Oh yes, they are, for mine is; and I don't like it, either."

"I don't like the way my mother tells me to fix my hair."
"Nor I," shouted another.
"I want to choose my own clothes, and my mother won't let me."

"I don't like the way my mother tries to look young when she really is old. I heard her tell someone she is thirty-seven! And I'd like to know if *that* isn't old."

"I wish my mother wouldn't come in and giggle when some of my boy friends stop by after school."

The girls were still going strong, but Lady thought that enough was enough, so she said:

"I think perhaps we have established the fact that mothers sometimes know how to irritate their daughters. Let's see now what we *like* in our mothers. Surely that shouldn't be too hard."

To Lady's surprise, there was absolute silence. Then one of the girls rose and said:

"Lady, you know we all do love our mothers. We do think they are wonderful. But please don't make us tell you what we like about them. That is so much harder."

That was an eye opener to Lady. She had thought that they would burst out with their likes even more quickly than with their dislikes. She had thought she knew girls pretty well, but she had learned something that night.

"I just want to talk to you a little bit about your mothers. I have met most of them; and I am a mother, too, you know. You are right in thinking that they are wonderful; and you are right when you say that they irritate you, for they do. Maybe you think that it should not be that way; but try as hard as a mother can, and she really does try, she rubs you the wrong way more often than the right at your age.

"There is nothing abnormal or strange about that. It is perfectly normal and natural. You are growing up. You don't want to be considered a little child any more. But that doesn't mean that it is all right for you to lose your temper and put on a scene when your mother suggests that you wear a dress that you dislike.

"Dr. Johnson has explained to you how and why you have so many conflicting emotions. One minute you are happy, the next you are down in the dumps, and then you flare up at the least little thing. In another few minutes, you are at peace with the world.

"It is hard to be your age. It is hard to grow up. Still, that is no reason to be uncontrolled. We all know men and women who

are married who act just like that, and what is the result? Broken homes and everyone unhappy. Now, right now, is the time that you can learn to get along with the man you are going to marry, even though you do not know who he is! You can do it by learning how to get along with your mother and father.

"I cannot command you to control yourselves. That would accomplish nothing. What I *can* do is to give a few suggestions that may help. When you are not feeling peeved about things, go over in your mind what it is that causes most friction between you and your mother. Probably clothes and the boys bring more heartaches than anything else.

"Just remember, she longs for you to look pretty. She longs for you to have the clothes that you like. She wants you to be popular. She saves her money to get you a dress; and when she buys it, she thinks you are going to love it. When you look at it and turn up your nose and refuse even to try it on, how do you think she feels? I grant that it may not be pretty. But can't you work out some way so that you can both be pleased? She is eager to help you. She really is; but she doesn't know how. Maybe you can think up a new plan for choosing your clothes.

"Try very hard to be patient with your mother if she does not seem to understand. You have been her little girl for such a long time. And then, all of a sudden, she finds that she has a young lady, and not a little girl any more to deal with. She can hardly believe that you are beginning to be interested in boys. Maybe her first impulse is to keep you from them. She may think you are too young to have dates or to go to parties.

"While she is learning to understand this new daughter of hers, she will be trying to meet you halfway. So if you don't get all that you want at first, wait a bit. She will come around herself; and then you will have so much more fun than if you have had to fight it out every time. She will be trying to get your point of view as you try to get hers. Every time that you and your mother can discuss things and work them out without hard feelings, just say to yourself, 'There now! I'm learning how to control myself so that when I get married, and my husband does something I don't like, I can just talk things over with him. I will not have to throw a book at him, the way they do in the movies!' There are no hard and fast rules entitled, 'How to get along with your mother!' *You* are a book. Your mother is another. You both have to study and learn."

Nell raised her hand. She wanted to speak.

"I think my mother is unreasonable. I am dead in love with a boy at school, and she says she does not like him."

"Are you 'going steady' with him?"

"Oh, no. I have never had a date with him. But every time I see him or think of him, I know I am in love. He is on the football team. I could just sit and sit and dream of him and do nothing else. He smiled at me once in the hall at school. Oh, Lady, he is marvelous!"

"Why doesn't your mother like him?"

"She just thinks I'm silly to talk about him so much."

"This is what I'd do, if I were you. I'd meet and talk with some of the other boys at school, and get your mind off of him a bit. Keep him as a sort of dream-man if you want to; but get a

few real ones into the picture. Your mother doesn't really dislike him, for she doesn't know him any more than you do!

"What she *does* object to (and I think wisely so) is for you to spend so much time just daydreaming. Talk to some other boys, and see if you don't think it is more fun to have a real boy friend than an imaginary one. Maybe one day you will meet this football hero of yours, and that will be all right too. But in the meanwhile, have a good time with others."

Another girl raised her hand.

"What's your question, Dot?"

"My mother does not want me to smoke, and yet *she* smokes all the time. Do you think she has a right to try to keep me from smoking?"

"You have opened up a pretty big subject, one I wish I had all the answers to. You know I do not smoke myself; so maybe I'm not the one to answer that question. Your mother is not telling you that you can *never* smoke. She does not want you to smoke *now*, while you are growing up.

"Whether it hurts her or not is an open question, with authorities on both sides, but no authority will say that it is good for either a teenage boy or girl to smoke. Probably some of you girls have taken a puff or two from a cigarette; but I am very sure that none of you have the habit, else you could not have stopped when you came to camp.

"Ask smokers who have tried to stop, and see how hard it is. I dare say that for one reason or another, your mother has tried to give up smoking herself, and maybe she did for a short time. But she was so uncomfortable while doing so, that she felt it

was not worth the effort, and so started it up again. I am not saying smoking is right or wrong for your mother. I *know* it is wrong for a girl your age.

"And it is something for you girls to think about before you start the habit. If you don't smoke, you save a lot of money that you can spend on pretty clothes. Then when you marry and your baby is on the way, you don't have to wonder if it is going to harm the baby then and during the nursing period. It is so much easier not to begin than it is to be told it is wise to give it up.

"As I said, I am not a smoker, and so do not know the pleasure that you'd think *must* come from it, or so many men and women would not smoke. It is something you girls will have to decide for yourselves. But one thing I am absolutely sure of is that it is wise for you to decide right now that you will not smoke until you are through high school."

More hands went up, but Lady looked at her watch and said, "We'll get together again for more questions another time. But right now, off to your cabins, every one of you!"

Chapter 10

THE MOTHERS TRY TO UNDERSTAND THEIR DAUGHTERS

Camp was in full swing, and Lady felt that she could slip off and speak in a nearby town where many of the girls lived. The meeting was held in the beautiful home of Mrs. Ellis. It was called to order. The gavel fell, and the president rose and said:

"This is the last meeting of the Woman's Club for the summer. I thought it would be most helpful if we had someone speak to us today on what we may expect from our teenage daughters when they return from camp. And don't we all shudder at the very thought! So I have invited Mrs. Rogers who has had much experience with the teen-agers to talk to us. Many of our daughters are in camp with her this summer. She is affectionately known as 'Lady' by the girls. And so, Mrs. Rogers,

the time is yours, and it goes without saying that you have an eager audience of mothers."

No wonder the girls were crazy about Lady. She was so pretty and beautifully dressed. She held herself well, and her hair was fixed just right. She had on lipstick, but exactly the right amount. Her dark navy blue suit was set off by a corsage. The mothers in the audience all envied her the easy time they felt she must have in managing her own two daughters. She certainly must know the answers to all their problems. So it came as a surprise when Lady began:

"First, I want to tell you that we are here to discuss a subject that no one knows any too much about; this is, how to be a wise mother to a teenage girl. The best we can do is to fumble along together and see if we cannot help each other with this age-old problem. It always comes as something entirely new when we wake up one morning and find we no longer have a little girl as a daughter, but instead, that much-talked-of-creature, a teen-ager. A feeling of helplessness comes over us.

"I wish all of our daughters were here unseen, so that they could hear us talk and so better understand us and our problems with them, for then they might realize that we are not ganging up against them to keep them down and prevent them from having a good time. We really want them to have fun, wear pretty clothes, and go out. There is so much talk about parents' understanding their children; but many is the time I've wished that children could understand their parents.

"Did you notice I said "children" when I was really thinking of the teen-agers? "Children" is a term we had better put out

of our thoughts and vocabulary at once. Yes, one minute they do act like children; and the next minute, we can hardly stand it if they want to look as if they were sixteen! Can you imagine what a turmoil of emotions must be going on within them when all of that is taking place?

"I need not ask what effect all of this is having upon us, their parents. We are so anxious to say and do the right thing, yet find ourselves in hot water all of the time doing and saying the wrong thing. We feel that the world of today is really against us, that never did parents face such problems. And we all feel that our particular daughter or daughters are the most unreasonable of all!

"Why is it that a girl can go off to the teenage club and have such a good time and then come home, kick over a chair, and fling herself upon her bed and sob? We want to comfort her, but she won't tell us what is the matter. Something so mysterious is taking place within her, that neither she nor anyone else can explain why. But, you say, we can't let this go on uncontrolled. We *must* discipline her somehow.

"Now comes the hardest pill for any mother to have to swallow. Your daughter has reached the age of rebellion. If you are wise, you will let someone else help you in your task. You will always remain her backlog of security. And mark my word, that is no small role, if only you are willing to play it.

"As you know, I am director of a camp for girls. You'd think that would be an ideal place for my own daughters. I tried having them there one summer. But never again! The next year off they went to a camp in another state. Why on earth they could

not have had that teenage adoration for me that the other girls had still irks me every time I think about it.

"Now why should this be? It is really not at all unreasonable. Our girls are growing up out of girlhood into womanhood. We mothers represent a bondage they don't like. We say "no" all too often, even if justifiably. They are thinking strange new thoughts they don't want to confide in us. But they must talk them over with someone–it may be with their girlfriends, it may be with some older woman.

"One day they're walking in the clouds. Everything goes well at school. They just love the dress we suggest; sometimes they may even give us a hug of approval. Next day, there's an outburst:

"I hate this dress. It's so short, and the awfullest shade of brown I ever saw. Whenever I wear it, I look as if I came from an orphanage. I just won't put it on!"

"It's snatched off, then trampled under her feet. And what does her mother say then? If she is wise, she will know that this is no time to discuss the clothes problem. She will go quietly out of the room while her stomach is fairly churning with emotion, half with anger and half with a feeling of utter inadequacy. But before leaving she will say, quietly:

"Bessie, pick out the dress that YOU want to wear today. Whatever it is, it will please me."

"Yes, I know what you are all thinking? '*That* is no way to discipline a daughter. If you give her an inch, she will take a mile next time.' Suppose she *does* take a mile and looks like a scarecrow as she goes to school? Don't think for one moment that she won't "get it" from her classmates. They will tell her

quickly enough that she is a sight. What *you* may say matters not, for she thinks *you* old-fashioned; but she is very anxious to be admired by her friends, though their taste is not yours.

"Another thing for us mothers to realize is that our daughters think that we are old in years as well as old in ideas. That is not easy for us to realize. No, we may not have a grey hair, and <u>the size of our dress may be fourteen.</u> We may be as youthful in our manner as can be; but the fact remains that, to the teen-ager, we are old.

"You can remember so clearly how you felt on *your* first date. It seems like yesterday. You can put yourself right into her life and feelings; you know (or at least you think you do!) exactly what she is going through. But to her, you live in an entirely different world.

"To begin with, you are married, and that alone is a terrible barrier. You remember so well being unmarried and how it felt. But she has no idea about the experiences of a married woman. And so we have to be very understanding and sympathetic with her if she seems unreasonable and fails to get our point of view.

"Yes, I know what you are all wishing–that I would tell you what to do about this boy business. There is so much freedom now, and the girls just seem wild. They chase the boys and telephone them, instead of waiting for *them* to ask for dates. We feel that they are just spoiling the boys, that they will soon begin to think that all they have to do is to sit back, and the girls will do the rest–buy tickets to the ball games and everything else. How can we get things back to normal once more, when the girls will be refined and the boys chivalrous?

"There is so much freedom now, and the girls just seem wild. They chase the boys and telephone them, instead of waiting for them to ask for dates. How can we get things back to normal once more, when the girls will be refined and the boys chivalrous?"

"Well, we will just have to admit that times have changed, and with them, our boys and girls. But let's not get too discouraged at the way things are today. Maybe this freedom we talk about is a good thing. It has woken us mothers up, and we realize as never before that the time has come when our girls, yes, our little girls, must know many things about life that we who were protected did not need to know.

"I have many of your girls in camp this summer, and I have had a very fine woman physician come and talk to them and tell them about "the facts of life," and answer every question honestly as they ask it. Every girl that leaves camp, I hope, will have a full realization about petting and what it may lead to, and a clear knowledge of the workings of her body. She will also have been told how boys differ from girls and why. They will at least know a little better why they feel and act as they do. More than this, I hope to instill in them an ideal of womanhood, for knowledge alone is not enough."

Just then, the telephone rang.

"It is for you, Mrs. Black."

The women instinctively stopped. They could not help but listen and hear:

"No, I don't think you had better go ... How do you know he is a good driver? ... Dear, that is a *very* old car ... What! *Eight* of you pile in? ... Well, be sure to get back before dark. You know your father ..." The conversation came to an abrupt end; and Mrs. Black returned to her seat with a worried expression on her face.

"Oh dear, what should I have done? Bill has just bought an old car." She did not have to say more, for every mother in the room knew what it was all about.

Some of the fathers had come down hard on their daughters and said, "You cannot." But that hadn't worked. It had only made matters worse. It produced more problems, instead of solving the first. There was an almost audible groan in the room, as they faced life with all their teen-agers. And at the

same time, the teen-agers were probably groaning over their unreasonable mothers!

But Lady somehow gave them hope.

"It really isn't quite as bad as all that," she smiled. "We'll all live through it somehow. There is getting to be a partnership between mothers and daughters as there never has been before. Mothers and daughters are trying to understand each other; and although there are still many clashes, now they are in the open and not behind our backs.

"No, this business of being a mother to a teenage girl isn't easy; nor is it easy for the teenage girl, either. Would you like to be one today? Not a single one of you would change places with her. Try hard to see the good things that she does; and even though you feel at times as if you could wring her neck, keep on praising her. One of these days you are going to hear her say, "'I have the most wonderful mother in all the world.'

"It may not come today, nor tomorrow; but it *will* come. Then you will feel a lump in your throat as you look at her in all her loveliness, and you will know that the effort was all worthwhile. Keep faith with her, that girl of yours. She is worth understanding."

The hostess rose. The meeting stood adjourned.

Chapter 11

WHAT AM I GOING TO BE WHEN I GROW UP?

It was raining outside, so the girls all went to the gym for their evening talk. Lady was there waiting for them. As soon as they were seated, she began:

"Many times this summer I have heard you girls discussing your future plans and asking one another:

"What are you going to be when you grow up?"

These have been some of your answers:

"Oh, I'm going in for nurses' training."

"I'm going to be a teacher."

"No, I'm going to take a secretarial course."

"Perhaps one or two of you have said you wanted to be a doctor, like Dr. Marilyn Johnson. Some of you will be sure to say:

"Oh, *I'm* going to get married," the tone of your voice rather implying:

"'I don't have to think about earning my own living or taking any special course with a husband to support me. If I know how to cook a little, that's all that will be necessary.' We'll consider all this in a little more detail.

"Once that may have been sound reasoning. But it very definitely is not true today. Frankly, I seriously doubt if that day ever returns. Not all of you will come out and say that you are going to get married, that it is your one ambition in life. In fact, some of you will state very definitely right now that you are *not* going to marry.

"But no matter what any of you plan in the way of a career, or a profession, or not being married, way down deep within you there is the desire for a home of your own; and you hope that some day your dream prince will come and take you to it. That is the way life is: You cannot escape it.

"However, you must not think that if you remain unmarried, as some of you undoubtedly will, you have failed. We can all point to women who have never married yet have done more toward helping others to succeed in life than many a married woman who has not thought of helping others. Just being married in no way spells success or happiness.

"Too many have leaped before they looked and then regretted it all the rest of their lives. Nor is divorce any way out, as so many boys and girls think it is. It may be justified, in certain cases; but it is a sign that someone has failed somewhere along the line. And none of us wants to be a failure.

"But let's go back to our problem: What do you want to be in life? Right now, this summer, you are preparing for your

career in the best possible way. For don't think for a minute that after you get your high school diploma, you've been handed a ticket for successful living. Instead, it's a milestone; better still, it's a springboard for bigger and better things. For unless your life has been well spent and filled to the brim and overflowing with every possible activity, in school and out, you will find yourself at a loss to know what to do when the day comes that we call Commencement.

"Believe it or not, that is why you are at camp–to learn how to live when you get out in the world. If you learn to play the game fair and square here, you will play it that way when you are at college or taking special training; and then, best of all, when you get married.

"We all want to be liked, to be popular. But no one achieves popularity by simply wanting it or by merely thinking about it. It is the girl who is so busy doing things and thinking of others, that has no time to wonder whether she is popular or not, who finds herself surrounded by the boys, and sought out by others who just like to be with her. She doesn't have to phone the boys for dates or sit by the phone whimpering and whining and not knowing what to do with herself.

"The girl who is going to succeed as a nurse, a teacher, a secretary or wife is the one that can excel in tennis, swimming and basketball, as well as in her school work. Above all, she is the girl who can get along with her friends and her family.

"I know perfectly well that girls of your age are very conscious of your looks. You all want to be pretty. That is all right; you should. But remember, it is not always the pretty face that

is really beautiful. I had a friend, when I was a girl, who was very homely. No one could deny that. She knew it; and she evidently determined that, because she was so homely, she would have to make up for it in other ways.

"She did not take the attitude that she was a 'nobody's darling' and sit back unloved. Instead, she realized that unless she offered something more to people, her looks would be a bar to her happiness. She worked hard at her studies, but she didn't stop there. She went into every school activity as well.

"Above all, she went out of her way to do something for everybody with whom she came in contact, whether that somebody was the janitor, a teacher, one of the girls, or a little child she happened to meet on the street.

"She was fortunate in having a keen sense of humor. She made a real effort to see to it that everyone had a good time at a party where she was a guest. Did she have dates? You may be sure she did. Today she is happily married, with a lovely family and home of her own.

"Let's pretend that one of you girls always feels inferior to other girls. You are convinced you can't possibly amount to anything when you grow up. You are constantly comparing yourself with girls who get better grades at school. At camp you see those who can excel in tennis or swim a little faster than you can. When you go to a party, you think that boys gather around them, and you are left a wallflower. You suffer more than more people think; for youth is not the happiest time of life. Perhaps an adult may say, "Oh, that is your age. You'll get over it."

"But it isn't much fun feeling all these feelings and thinking all these thoughts. You want to be like other girls–attractive, popular and successful.

"Let me tell you a secret. Those other girls that you are envying are feeling and thinking very much as you are. They don't know what they are going to be or do when they grow up, either. They may be able to swim and play tennis better than you, but instead of being happy over that, they feel they can't stand it because they are so poor in craft work or tap dancing, and you are so good at it. Maybe you didn't think of that.

"And now what about you at a party? You think the other girls are having the time of their lives because you see them in the midst of a group of boys. Perhaps one of those girls looks over at you and sees you talking to just one boy. And what does *she* think? 'Oh dear, I wish I were Alice [we'll call you Alice]. She is talking to the only boy here that I want to be with. I just know he is going to like her better than he does me.' Is she happy at the party? Utterly miserable. She thought *you* were having a good time, and you thought *she* was.

"I'll have to admit there are some girls who always have a group of boys buzzing around them. They have "personality plus," or "umph," or "it," or whatever you choose to call it. But I am not going to admit that they are the most fortunate or the happiest and most to be envied. Girls are often misled by this teenage popularity, and so they do not put forth the effort which it is going to take to be the really worthwhile woman every girl wants to be. It is hard for you to realize that one day you will be grown up and actually called a woman. That is a

dreamy, hazy future state, and perhaps none too attractive at the moment. You don't care ever to be like the average woman you know; but there are a few that you admire and want to be like. Think of them.

"Let's look at a few of the things you do here that will give you the full life that you all want, a life of interest in many lines, and one that can help you to adjust to new interests later on. It is the eager mind that counts, the mind that keeps on learning always. Wouldn't it be a terrible thing if when you left camp you were to take away only what you had been taught here, and never cared to go out after new knowledge?

"You play tennis here and swim, though you may never need those activities later on. The big purpose of all our physical activities is to train your bodies to be healthy, well formed and capable of carrying on the work that you will be doing some day. No matter what it is, you will need to be strong and attractive physically. You certainly want your keen mind to be housed in a beautiful body. Not one single day can be neglected; for every day you lay one brick in the foundation of the house you are to live in called 'yourself.'

"Now suppose you make some big mistake. Maybe you've told a lie, or maybe you've said some very mean, unkind thing. Maybe you have let a boy go a little farther than you wish you had. It may not have been anything really wrong; but anyhow, it preys on your mind. What are you going to do about it?

"First of all, let's realize that we all make mistakes. None of us go through life without doing something that we wish we had not done. That is part of this world of ours. But one mistake

need not lead to another. We can learn by our mistakes and sometimes climb up higher in helping others not to make the same ones. There is one thing that never, never helps. That is to brood, to keep thinking and thinking and feeling that you did wrong. Perhaps what you did wasn't so serious, after all. If you ever have that guilty feeling which is such a handicap to success, talk it over with some older person. If not your mother, then your doctor, your pastor or your teacher. The mere telling of it may make the whole thing disappear, and you will say to yourself, 'How silly I was to worry over that!' It will make you feel so good to get it out of your system. Keep reminding yourself that what you suffer and feel is not 'just you,' but that everyone is feeling like that, in one way or another.

"So far this evening we have talked about what you want to *be* when you grow up, the kind of girl that can make a success in life. There is not one of you here that does not have something in mind that you want to *do*, but you change from one thing to another; and that is the way it should be, right now. One day you may think you want to be an artist, the next day you are sure you want to be a movie star or a model in New York. Even the Army or Navy may appeal; or one of the good old stand-bys, teaching or nursing.

"Never have girls had such wonderful opportunities. Now they may enter practically any field open to men. It has been proved beyond doubt that we are not inferior creatures, that we can compete successfully with men in just about everything. Now whether you want to enter some of these masculine fields is a different matter. Right here comes a

most important decision that you will have to make later on. Choose the training that *you* want, not what anybody else wants for you.

"Never have girls had such wonderful opportunities. Now they may enter practically any field open to men. It has been proved beyond doubt that we are not inferior creatures, that we can compete successfully with men in just about everything."

"The other day I saw a cartoon that was very suggestive of the changing world of today. A teenage girl said to her mother, "I think he is getting serious. Last night he told me he thought it was time that I was getting a job!"

"Now what did that cartoon teach? Just this. The day has passed when a pretty face is enough to attract a man when he is looking for a wife. It may still fool some people, but they often live to regret it. Being trained so as to be self-supporting is an insurance policy that should be a requisite for every wife, whether she ever uses it or not. After all, homemaking as a profession is a full-time job, surpassed by none in its importance; but it is inspiring indeed to see young couples today sharing in work so that they can make both ends meet, and in that way establish a home. And it is just as inspiring to see the young husband share in the housework and in caring for the baby. Together they move forward.

"There is a wonderful thing about growing up and planning your life at your age. What you do day by day is what counts. Each day is so very important. Right now in camp, and when you go back to school, you are becoming the girl of your dreams, and, yes, the girl that some boy will dream of, too, and one day will claim as his own.

"Girls, you have been very good tonight to listen so attentively. For what I have been saying is not easy to understand, and it's very hard to put into practice. But I believe that my girls can do it; and, what is more, will do it.

"Our camp season is flying, so make the most of it. Good night."

Chapter 12

FRIENDSHIPS

A few evenings later, the girls, gathered for the customary discussion, listened with even more than their usual attention as Lady began speaking:

"Let's talk a little bit more about the boys tonight. Not that we haven't mentioned them before! But this time, we want to think about the kind of a boy each one of you would like to have as a friend, if you could make him to order. Some of you have boy friends now; others will have them next year. There are a great many boys in high school and a great many different kinds, so you'll have a wide variety to pick from. Maybe you think *they* should be the ones to pick *you*! Yes, they will. But you'll have a choice, too, as to which ones you want to be with.

"I know it is quite the fashion these days for boys and girls to pair off. You want to feel that you really own the boy you are going with, at least for the time being; and you quite resent the idea of another girl's cutting in and perhaps cutting you out! This is often a time of heartache for a girl, even at your age. But if you will look at things sensibly now and plan for them in

advance, maybe you can avoid having some of those hard feelings and enjoy being with boys, or *a boy*, next year.

"You all know, of course, that you are definitely *not* at the age to get married. Then at what age are you? You are at the perfect age for meeting boys, so that you can really know them; and know their good traits, yes, and their bad ones, too. You want to study yourselves, and learn what it is that makes you prefer one boy to another, and why one boy is liked by girls but isn't popular with the boys. Yes, one of the most important studies you'll take in high school is BOYS.

"Your teachers may not agree with me in this. For you know you do drive them crazy at times because they feel that you are thinking too much about the boys. That may well be true in the case of many a girl, for there is nothing gained by just mooning around and daydreaming. That isn't studying boys. That's making a fool of yourself, and depriving yourself of the opportunity of getting ahead with your education or of planning for some good times at a club meeting or game.

"I've already talked to you about the good times boys and girls can have together in a school play, a club, games and other activities. The more you can be together in groups, the more fun and good times you'll have–and the more boys you'll learn to know.

"But at every party there are always some who are going to want to slip off and go to a car and pet. You'll see more of that next year than you did last, for you'll be a year older. Many of the girls who'll be slipping off with the boys have not been told what you've heard from Dr. Marilyn Johnson this summer and so do

not know the risk they are running. What they thought was going to be a little fun may prove to be far from fun for some of them, when they have had time to think things over the next day.

"I hate to say it, but it's not always the *boy* who is the one that suggests going out to the car. All too often, it is the girl. But I have great faith in you girls; I really believe you have learned your lesson about petting and what it may lead to. I feel confident that you are prepared now to meet any situation in which you may find yourselves and act in such a way that you can be proud of yourselves. You'll find that the boys will respect you in a way you have no idea of. Is that old-fashioned, for a boy to respect a girl for doing what is right? *No*—a thousand times no! You are still the ones to lead and set the pace when it comes to setting up ideals and living up to them.

"I read an article the other day lamenting what seems to me a very serious state of affairs, if it is true. It said that girls had become so lax, and were so free in their conduct, that the time had come for the boys to call a halt to this sort of thing and set an example for the girls! If that can be said, we have come to a sad time indeed.

"It will not be true, however, if a group of girls like you determine to hold to your motto, *"It's smart to go straight!"* Even one girl alone can exert a tremendous influence; and I don't mean one little pious prig of a girl, either. I mean the May Queen type. And if one girl alone can change things so at school, just think of what a group of such girls as you can do!

"Speaking of May Queens, there was a study made of the social lives of the girls who had been chosen as May Queen in one

of our large state universities. They looked into the social and personal life of each girl chosen by the student body for this important position for each of the five preceding years, to see what type of girls they represented. There was not one girl that was known as a heavy petter! As you know, they were picked out from among hundreds of students and had to be voted upon by the boys as well as by the girls. That certainly proved something that it is well for every girl to think over seriously. No, petting is *not* one of the requirements for popularity or friendship, but quite the reverse. And again I say that you need not act like a touch-me-not, either.

"Well, if petting is not one of the requirements for popularity or friendship with a boy, what is? I believe I would put common interests first on my list. But listen to me–this is a secret for you to hear, but not to tell. Suppose there is a boy you like a lot, but you can't stand his hobby, stamp collecting. He is simply wrapped up in it. You can fool him!

"Get busy and learn a little about stamps. Maybe a friend who has a correspondent in some foreign country will occasionally let you have one from a letter just received. Another acquaintance who finds out that you are interested may give you a rare one. Before you know it, you are as excited over stamps as your boy friend is; and you are having the best time together after school going over his album with him. And the more stamps you get for him, why there you are with a good friend. And he never knew that you didn't like stamps!

"Perhaps you know a boy who seems to want to go fishing all his spare time, while you wouldn't go for anything. Still, there

"But listen to me—this is a secret for you to hear, but not to tell. Suppose there is a boy you like a lot, but you can't stand his hobby, stamp collecting. He is simply wrapped up in it. You can fool him! Get busy and learn a little about stamps."

is something mighty nice about him, and you like to be with him, and you hope that maybe he won't want to go fishing *all* his life. You may have something there; but don't sit down and wait for that day to come!

"Send for a catalog of fishing tackle and sporting equipment. Find out about what fish have been taken from his favorite lake or stream. Get an interesting yarn about some old fisherman or fishing village, and bring it into the conversation. Maybe this boy is rather shy and a little bit afraid of girls.

But when he sees that you are interested in the same things he is, he will open up and talk. You may be amazed at the good books he has read that you can talk about. And presto, you have him as a friend!

"No, there is no need for any girl not to have a boy friend. She may not have boys buzzing around her as some girls do. But after all, when the great day comes and the wedding bells are ringing, it is only one man that counts. But of course the first boy friend you have is not usually the one for that occasion. You want to meet and know a lot of boys, to make sure that you are making no mistake. So you study boys and see how many you can attract as friends, now that you're in high school, by just finding out their interests, getting interested yourself, and helping them with their hobbies.

"It is quite an art in itself, this business of getting a boy friend and holding him after you get him. There is nothing else quite as fascinating at your age. But if you find that it is absorbing too much of your time or thoughts, keeping you from your studies or from joining in school activities with a real zest, then shoot up a little red flag in your brain as a danger signal, and get back to other things.

"For a strange thing about all this is that when girls show they are too anxious to attract the boys, they lose a lot of their appeal. A boy is far more likely to choose the girl who is not "boy crazy," than he is to want the girl who is.

"One other word of advice. Think twice before you let yourself become the "aggressive girl." Boys don't like to be run after, as a rule, even though some of them may act as if they didn't mind.

They still like to be the ones to ask for dates. That doesn't mean that you have to sit back and let the other girls get ahead of you, while you take the attitude that you don't care. You do care; and you should. And I can almost promise you that if you always look your prettiest, show your interest in some boy and his hobby, yet stay in with your group, you'll have a boy friend; and he'll be followed by another, and maybe by still another, as it should be at your age. If I were talking to a group of college-age girls who are seriously considering marriage, I might give entirely different advice. But to you teen-agers, it's a case of "the more, the merrier" when it comes to having boy friends.

"But they are not the only friends you'll make. The girl who just runs around with boys and says she doesn't like girls is far from being the attractive person she wishes she were. She is not liked particularly by either boys or girls. Friendships formed now between you girls may go with you right through life. Of course a girl who is congenial with you now may not be congenial in a few years; and the same is true with your boy friends. But the possibility of making lifelong friends is one of the big reasons for coming to camp.

"I don't mean crushes, where two girls "love each other to death," or where a camper "simply adores" her counselor. These are all right at your age. But sometimes you see two girls who, as they grow older, want to be with each other exclusively. They don't want each other to have friends among either boys or other girls.

"If you suspect yourself of developing such an interest in another girl, no matter how fine both of you may be, then watch

out! You might be entering into what the psychologists call an 'unwholesome friendship.' It doesn't take any great knowledge of human nature to see that such a friendship is far from desirable. For every girl should want the companionship of boys; and, too, want the companionship of one special boy as she gets to the age when she naturally should be thinking of marriage.

"After a girl has had too close and exclusive a friendship with another girl, she may find it very hard to grow into the capacity for friendship and love with the other sex.

"So keep your friendships with boys and with girls on a high level of companionship, working together and playing together, and learning how to get along with each other. You may not realize it; in fact, you may never have thought of such a thing; but it is true that in that way, you will be laying the strongest possible foundation for a happy home of your own, when the right time comes along in the not-so-very-distant future."

Chapter 13

WHAT DOES GRANDMA THINK?

"Grandma, did you have fun when you were my age?" asked Helen. She had run over to the dining hall where her grandmother was a dietitian and had stopped for a chat. Evidently, Lady's talk the night before had made a deep impression upon her.

"Well, let me see," replied Grandma. "Of course I did have fun. But somehow, as I think back, I can remember more times when I was miserable than when I was happy. To begin with, my mother and I never *could* see eye to eye about my clothes. In those days, when a girl was twelve, the length of her skirt began to get longer and longer with each new dress until she was sixteen, when it reached to her ankles."

"Oh, Grams! What a sight you must have been!"

"Yes. But each inch added meant that you were that much more grown up. We didn't buy our dresses in those days but had a dressmaker come to the house and make them. I can

remember *begging* my mother to make my dress just a little bit longer than she thought best. She gave in to me, and it came almost to the middle of my leg.

"When I wore it to school, the girls all hooted at me and wanted to know who I thought I was trying to look like–the teacher or somebody? I couldn't get home fast enough after school. I threw myself across the bed and cried and cried."

"Why, Grandma, that was the craziest thing I ever heard of to be worried over. I would never have let that bother me."

"Well, my dear, maybe you wouldn't. But didn't I hear your mother and you discussing your evening dress? Your mother wanted straps over the shoulders, and you said in no uncertain terms that the girls would laugh at you if you wore that kind of a baby-looking dress."

"But, oh, Grams, you *know* that is different." And Helen jumped up out of her chair. Her face was flushed, and she looked as if she were just ready for a fight. "You *know* that is different. The way I look in an evening dress is very important. I want the boys to like me, and they won't if I look like a little girl, the way Mother wants me to look."

"You see," her grandmother said quietly, "you and I were not so very different when we were fourteen, after all. We were both trying our best to look grown up, and our mothers were trying their best to hold us back. I guess that's the way life is supposed to be, and then we strike a happy medium when we grow up."

"But Mother never had anything to worry about when she was my age. Daddy says she was always beautiful and always

knew exactly what to say and do. She never did anything wrong when she went to a party."

"Now, listen to me," answered Grandma. "That may be what your father remembers. But *I* can remember something very different. I shall never forget the time I bought your mother the prettiest pink dress with little rosebuds all over it. She looked darling in it. But did she like it? No! She said she wouldn't be seen with such a dress on. She wanted plain satin.

"We didn't have much money in those days, and I had bought the rosebud dress at a big sacrifice. But I couldn't bear to see her so unhappy, so I took it back and got the pink satin. And what do you think? One of the girls at the party had on that very rosebud dress, and everyone said she was beautiful, while your mother felt like the ugly duckling! She didn't have one bit of a good time."

"Why, Grandma," exclaimed Helen in amazement, "I never *dreamed* that Mother ever gave you any trouble!"

"It all just goes to show that your age is a hard age to live through, no matter what, whether a hundred years ago or a hundred years from now. Every boy and every girl seems to have to live through what is known as 'growing pains.' Some suffer more than others, but all suffer."

"I never thought of that before," said Helen, slowly and thoughtfully. "Isn't there some way in which a person can be happy *all* the time?"

"No. In this old world of ours, that is a state no one is in all the time. Life has its ups and downs. Perhaps people your age can go down deeper and then rise higher than at a later age.

But we all have to learn to get along while we are unhappy as well as when we are happy. My mother used to tell me that years ago, and you will be telling it to your children years from now. You think that over, and we'll talk more about it sometime.

"But do tell me right now, Grandma, whatever happened when you were crying on your bed because your skirt was too long?" inquired Helen, as her grandmother paused.

"Well, my mother let me cry for a little while, and then she said, 'Let's look at your dress. I can shorten it an inch or two right now, and it will look much better, I'm sure.' She didn't even say, 'I told you so.' She just made me feel good all over. And when I went to school the next day the girls all thought it looked perfect."

A week or so passed, and Helen came by to talk with her grandmother again. This time she was just on the verge of tears.

"Oh, Grandma," she burst out. "I had an awful time at the party last night. One of the boys was sitting beside me. I had my hand in my lap, and we sat there talking. He slipped his hand over mine and gave it a little squeeze.

"I snatched it away with a jerk, and he said, 'All right, if that's the way you feel, I'll go.' Then he jumped up and left me. I like him *so* much. He is one of the nicest boys I've met in a long time. I don't know why I acted like that. Oh, dear, oh, dear, he'll *never* speak to me again, I know. What *shall* I do?" and Helen started to cry as if her heart would break.

Her grandmother remained quiet for a minute or two. Then she said, "Let me tell you what happened to me one time when I was a year or two older than you are now, for in Grandma's

day, we didn't go out with the boys the way you do now. I was sixteen before I ever 'went with' a boy–we didn't say 'date' in those days.

"This boy walked home with me from church in broad daylight. Was I thrilled! My heart beat fast when he asked me if I would play tennis with him. He called for me the next afternoon, and we walked to the park together to play. After the game, he suggested that we sit under a tree and rest. I made quite sure we were two feet apart so nobody would talk about us.

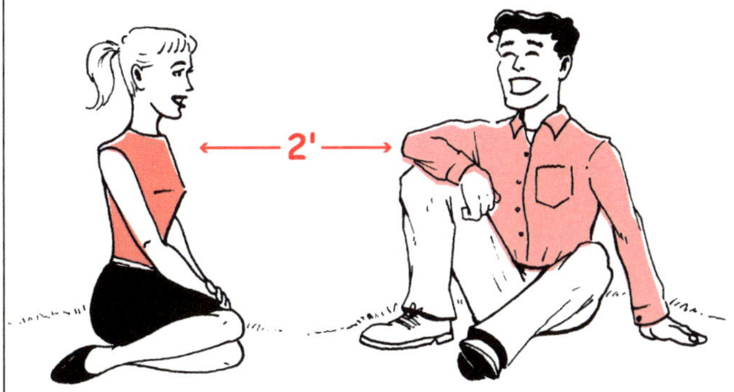

"After the game he suggested that we sit under a tree and rest. I made quite sure we were two feet apart so nobody would talk about us.

"He began to get a little closer. I thought I would just about die if somebody should see us."

"He began to get a little closer. I thought I would just about die if somebody should see us. At that moment, a friend of my mother's happened to walk by. To this day I can live over how I felt."

"But Grandma! What difference could that possibly make?" asked Helen, completely mystified.

"Why, I thought she would tell my mother, and my mother would think I was doing something I ought not to be doing."

"Well, I must say you certainly lived in a funny time if things like that bothered you."

"But wait a minute," Grandma continued. "He asked me if he could write to me when he went off to college. I told him no, because I thought it wouldn't be proper to say yes at the very first, though I was just dying to have him write me so that I could show his letters to the girls.

"Well, we played another set of tennis, and then we went home, and he never asked again to write to me. Oh, how I suffered! Oh, how I wished I had only said yes! But he did write, after all, so all that agony was for nothing. He was probably suffering, too, thinking he shouldn't have asked to write to me. For just remember, boys can feel that they have made fools of themselves just as much as girls.

"Do you know what psychologists call that feeling? They call it the 'inferiority complex.' All of us, young and old, have it, and we have to fight it off. But somehow at your age it hurts the most. You feel that you are the only one who is always doing the wrong thing, saying what you shouldn't, that you are not popular, that everybody else looks better than you do and has a much better time at parties.

"In other words, you just feel sorry for yourself. You don't enjoy being that way the least little bit, but you can't seem to help it. At times you feel that you don't rate with the boys as much as the other girls do, and that makes you want to stay at home, away from the crowd, instead of being one of them."

"That's just exactly the way I feel, Grandma. What can I do to be popular?"

"First of all, remember this, and keep saying it over and over again to yourself. Every boy and girl in your class is feeling the same way, no matter how they act. Each one is putting on a bold front to hide how inferior he really feels. Do you realize that there are boys in your class who want you to like them ever so much, only they don't know how to go about getting you to like them? They feel that they say and do the wrong things every time they are with you.

"It isn't going to be easy for you to follow my suggestion. But you just try this, the next time you are in a group of boys and girls. Pick out some boy that you know is awkward and self-conscious. Maybe he has pimples on his face and feels that he is ugly and unpopular. As you pass by him, make some comment that will make him feel good. You might say, 'My, I wish *I* could get the good grades in English that you do.' Or you might comment of how good-looking his necktie is, or make some equally trivial remark. But to him it would mean something tremendous that a girl as fine as you even noticed him.

"You wouldn't have to date him or anything like that. But if you could make him feel comfortable for even a few minutes, that would be well worthwhile. If you just keep looking for

things you can do or say to the boys and girls in school or camp who don't have your charm, you will soon find yourself forgetting your own troubles."

"But, Grandma, you *know* you don't think I have charm. Or do you, really?" asked Helen, in evident surprise.

"Why of course I do. You are one of the prettiest girls in camp, and everybody seems to like you."

"But most of the time I think nobody likes me," replied the girl, still not convinced.

"If you'll try my little trick of trying to make some of your friends feel more popular, you won't have to wonder whether you are popular or not. You won't be wondering whether you have on the prettiest dress to make you attractive. You'll be sought after by boys and girls alike. Now dry your tears and run along, dear. Don't forget you are tops. Grandma is proud of you. Have fun these last days of camp."

The bugle sounded, and Helen ran off to the water front.

Chapter 14

THE GIRLS ASK QUESTIONS

Lady and Dr. Marilyn Johnson were seated by the council fire as the girls filed down to their seats. Each dropped a question into a basket which had been placed on the ground. It seemed about to overflow. Unimportant and even silly as some of these questions might seem to people who did not understand girls, many of them concerned vital problems. Certainly, each deserved a thoughtful answer, and each would receive such treatment. The first to be picked out of the basket read as follows:

"I never seem to know what to talk about when I am with a boy. I act sort of stupid. Please tell me what to say."

Dr. Johnson turned with a smile to Lady as if that were for her, and Lady began:

"Of course I don't know who asked this question. But whoever she is, I want to tell her first of all that she is far from stupid, else she would not be asking this very sensible question. She

isn't alone in this. Lots and lots of girls are just like her in this particular situation.

"As for not being able to talk with a boy because she can't think of anything to say, many an adult is just like her. Let me tell you the secret of success in conversation. Ask the boy one or two questions about himself, and then let *him* do the talking! You need hardly say a word, but look and act very much interested in what he is telling you. If he gets stuck, help him out a little bit by asking another question. Then do you know what

"But in the meantime, go to your doctor, and follow his directions carefully. He will tell you exactly how to cleanse your face and whether to use any medicine. Above all, he will instruct you about the use of makeup."

he will say about you? 'I know one girl that I enjoy dating. She is so easy to talk to. She knows just what to say.' Try that little trick, and see how it works."

Another slip of paper: "My face is so covered with pimples, I'm ashamed to go out anywhere. They make me look so ugly. Can I do anything to get cured?"

Dr. Johnson was most sympathetic with this questioner, for it happened that she had a daughter who was suffering from the same complaint. So she spoke with real feeling:

"I know exactly how you feel and how you are suffering. But remember that there are many, many other girls–and boys, too–who are going through the same experience at your age. For much of your trouble comes from the over-activity of the glands of the skin; that is one of the signs of commencing adulthood. Much of this trouble will disappear as you get older.

"But in the meantime, go to your doctor, and follow his directions carefully. They will differ according to whether your skin is over dry or over oily. He will tell you exactly how to cleanse your face and whether to use any medicine. Above all, he will instruct you about the use of makeup. Don't be tempted to try to cover up by using heavy makeup, which will clog the pores and make things worse. I'm sure he'll warn you against eating candy, and especially chocolate candy, and against sweet, carbonated drinks.

"Never take the attitude that because your skin shows a few blemishes, you might as well give up and not try to look your best. Bear in mind constantly that there is much more to being beautiful than having a pretty face. Your expression, the

light that shines in your eyes, your sympathetic attitude, your thoughtful little ways; in fact, your whole personality will more than make up for any blemishes in the eyes of the boy you are interested in, or of anyone else, for that matter.

"It often happens that a girl who suffers a little because of some such handicap develops something within herself that is very appealing. Haven't you heard people say, 'Oh yes, she's pretty enough; but there's nothing there'? She has relied on that pretty face and has not done anything to create real beauty. I would say to the girl who asked this question:

"Do all that you can to improve your complexion; and then forget it to the best of your ability, and join in with your group in all of its activities. You will be amazed to find how few of them, whether boys or girls, notice what you think is the first thing they see. No, they want *you*, not your perfect complexion.

"This story illustrates my point. A girlhood friend of mine had very prominent, ugly 'buck' teeth. She felt that everybody noticed these when she was introduced. She was so conscious of them that she was certain the boys would never go with her. But they did, and she married. Yet she had made a perfect bug-a-boo of those teeth; they still bothered her. The fact that her husband felt that she was foolish to worry about them didn't help at all. So she finally decided to do something about them.

"She went off on a so-called 'vacation' and had something done to her teeth. I don't know just what the operation was; but somehow or other, they were no longer prominent. She was delighted. How different life would be for her now!

"She came back, expecting everyone to comment on her improved looks. To her utter amazement, nobody noticed the change! Nobody told her how much better she looked. 'Well,' she said to herself, 'if only I could have learned this lesson years ago, how much suffering I'd have been spared!'

"I suppose every one of you girls has something about you that you feel is a handicap. Some of you think you are too tall, others that they are too short. Some of you hate your hair and feel that there's nothing you can do about it. I know you must have noticed that I have a scar on my cheek from an accident I had as a child. That used to worry me terribly till after I had grown up; I found that it made no difference to anybody but myself. All of us have something we don't like. Let's remedy it if we can, and then forget it and think of helping the other fellow."

The next question was for Lady: "*I* think it is all right for a girl to telephone a boy for a date. If the boys didn't like it, they would not make dates that way. I think they like to be invited by a girl and have their way paid to a movie. What makes our mothers think they don't?"

The girls enjoyed this question immensely and laughed merrily. Lady enjoyed it, too, though at first she did not seem quite sure what to say. After a moment's thought, she began:

"There's a lot of truth to what you say. I'll try to help you see your mothers' objections. We all know that social customs change with every generation. This is certainly true with boys and girls and dating. Your grandmother never went to a concert (there were no movies in her day) without a chaperone sitting beside her and her 'escort,' for that is what they

used to call her date. And she had to be home by ten o'clock at night, too!

"She was told nothing about the physical workings of her body, or of the boy's. That was something she must never so much as hear mentioned. She knew nothing about such things before she married. She was protected in every possible way. She was never permitted to be alone with a man; and so, her elders thought, nothing that was wrong could happen to her.

"Now your mothers had more freedom than that, but nothing like what you have today. Never, I suppose, has there been an age where there has been as much freedom and equality between boys and girls. It is a wonderful age for you girls to live in. But it means that a tremendous responsibility has been thrown on your shoulders. Your grandmothers never had any of it; and your mothers, only a little.

"You have to take your place in the world, but you must be fortified with every possible bit of knowledge about what folks used to call 'the facts of life,' for no chaperone will sit by your side at the movies or ride with you in a car at night. It's up to you to know just how to conduct yourselves. It is possible that too much responsibility has been given you. I just don't know. But I *do* know that that is life today, and you must take it as you find it. This is just by way of introduction. Now let's get back to the question of the girl who's asking about telephoning a boy for a date.

"Yes, the girl who does that does get dates. And maybe some of the boys like it that way. But if you could ever hear the mothers of the boys you telephone talk about those girls

who are always calling up their sons and the comments the boys make about them, you'd see that lots of boys still like girls who aren't too forward and eager to get them. I'll have to admit that many a boy has been caught by just those methods. But I don't believe it's the way that leads to the happiest courtship and marriage.

"I think the give and take between boys and girls today is fine. It's a big step toward a better understanding. I believe it's a good thing for a group of teen-agers to go to the movies and each pay for his own ticket. Otherwise, you could not begin to have the fun together that you do. But if a boy wants to pay you a little courtesy because you are the girl, let him do it. There are those little things that do not cost him money at all, like being thoughtful and considerate and polite. Make it easy for him to be a gentleman. One day, when you are a little bit older, you will appreciate those little thoughtful ways. He has to learn, and you girls can help him."

Another piece of paper was drawn from the basket: "I'd like to ask a physical question. Should I go in swimming when I'm having my period?" Dr. Johnson answered at once:

"I believe the best medical authorities agree that it is best to stay out of very cold water at that time, even though you will see advertisements that say that you need make no difference in your daily life because of this. I also feel that there should be no horseback riding or very strenuous exertion of any kind, like hiking or mountain climbing, especially for the first day or two. About other exercises such as tennis or golf, you can let your feelings be your guide. Individuals differ in this respect.

"Right here I'd like to put in a little word about refinement. There is so much freedom in the world today that we sometimes forget that we don't have to talk about a thing just because we happen to know about it–and especially to the boys. You have been taught all about your physical development and that of the boys, and they have been told about you. They know that a girl has her periods, of course; but that is no reason why you should discuss the subject with them, as some girls have been known to do.

"Let's bring back a little of the refinement of other days, without the ignorance that marked them. You girls want to attract boys who will appreciate those little touches of gentility. There are still the niceties of life in this changing world of ours. And there are plenty of people of the better sort who look for them, are glad when they see them, and are disappointed at their lack."

The next question made the girls sit up and listen expectantly to Dr. Johnson's answer. It read:

"I once saw a sign that said 'Clinic for Social Diseases.' What did that mean? I asked one of the girls at school, and she said it was for bad people, folks who had done something wrong. But she didn't know, either. Can you tell us?"

"This is a question," Dr. Johnson replied slowly, "that I should like to avoid answering. But even if you hadn't asked it, I should have felt that I ought to bring up the subject. For you girls must know the facts, the bad as well as the good, if you are to be safe in this world.

"There are certain diseases that are known as the 'social diseases' because they are usually, although not always, the direct result of immoral association between men and women.

You probably have heard that most states require a physical examination for a man and a woman who want to marry so as to make sure that neither of them has a disease with which the other one might become infected.

"We'll have time for just one more question. Let's have the last one:"

"I always feel that everything I do is the wrong thing; and it makes me so unhappy. I say the wrong thing to boys; I say the wrong thing to my teachers. Then I wish I hadn't! What can I do about that?"

"Now, let me tell you something, whoever asked that question," said Lady, earnestly. "What you said to the boys, or to your teachers, probably wasn't the wrong thing at all. The fact that you think it was doesn't make it so. Many girls are overly sensitive at your age. It is a fine trait, in moderation, for it keeps you from hurting people's feelings. But you've gotten just a bit too sensitive, or critical of yourself.

"I know you girls get tired of hearing us older folks keep saying 'at your age this,' and 'at your age that.' But for these few years that you are living through right now, many things happen to you for just that reason. You do have feelings now 'at your age' that you won't have a little later. So be patient with yourselves, and don't let it worry you if you are hypersensitive about many things. And one of these is the thing you have just asked about; that is, thinking you have said or done the wrong thing, when you really haven't."

Dr. Marilyn Johnson and Lady rose together and stood smiling their goodnight, while the girls broke up into groups and walked away talking earnestly together.

Chapter 15

THE LAST CAMPFIRE

Lady was looking her best. The girls always thought she was beautiful; but for the last campfire, she seemed to stand a little straighter, and her hair was fixed so that it seemed just a little softer. She was lovely, as the light from the fire lit up her face.

"I never come to the last campfire of the season without a lump in my throat, and I know each one of you girls is feeling the same way. But we are all going to swallow that lump. There are to be no tears, neither now nor when you go to your cabins. After all, this is just another day in camp; and after we leave tomorrow, most of us will be seeing each other all through the winter. And so we are going to be sensible–at least for once in our lives!

"I thought it would be fitting to run over a few of the things we have talked about this summer and get them clearly in our minds. At the very beginning of camp, we decided that we would study ourselves, as we had never done before. We would learn about ourselves, emotionally and physically, and then see if we could not get along better with ourselves and with other people.

"We learned that we all go through a certain number of emotional stages. Each stage is important, and we take along with us through life some of the characteristics of each period of development. But there is always a danger that somewhere along the journey between babyhood and womanhood that we might stop and stay too long at one stage. For example, it is natural for little girls to want to play only with little girls. But if at twenty-one there was no interest in wanting to be with men and desiring marriage, then they have been what psychologists call "fixated" at the little girl stage. You want to live to the fullest degree every stage of emotional development, so that when you are grown, you can take your place in the world a mature woman, eager for the responsibilities of womanhood. If you know these things, you can help yourselves to grow up.

Dr. Marilyn Johnson has made perfectly clear to you the differences between boys and girls–and between men and women–why their bodies are alike in so many ways, and yet so very different.

"We have had it very forcibly brought to us that all these new physical developments that come at adolescence bring new driving forces within us that are not always easily kept under control. Petting increases the physical desires and so should be avoided. Only in marriage should there by any physical relationship between a boy and a girl, or a man and a woman. I know all my girls have made that decision already, for I know very well that each of you wants a happy home with children. You want the deep and lasting love of your husband.

"Maybe Dr. Johnson and I have seemed a little cold and dictatorial about the girl and boy relationship in high school. You may think that we have left the romantic age behind us so long ago that we forget what it is to have your heart beat fast when a certain boy looks at you. Some of you are going to feel before you leave school that you are old enough to love and be loved, and that you are at the perfect age for romance, else you would not be so stirred by moonlight, or a love song over the radio.

"Not one of you girls here tonight can believe in love and romance more than I do. In fact, I might even say *as much* as I do. I know what it means in reality, while so far, you can only dream of it! There is nothing as important in life as love, the early love affairs, and those that mature later from friendships into a deep and lasting comradeship through life. Down through the ages, poets have sung about love; and every great story is often great because of its love theme. This summer I have tried not to minimize love, but to emphasize it, so that you can begin to prepare yourselves right now for the great experience of romance that awaits you. You will not always find it easy, for nothing in life that is really worthwhile is easily won; but the goal is certainly worth striving for.

"You have learned, I hope, this summer to understand your mothers better, to appreciate their efforts to help you, even if you feel that they are not always right. You have learned that in life there is a give and take of ideas, in order that we may live well together; and talking things over is far better than becoming emotional, losing our tempers and saying things we'll wish we had not said.

"Do you know that mothers (and fathers, too, for that matter) need not only to be understood by their daughters, but they need to be appreciated? You think so many lovely thoughts about them; but do you always tell it to them? Many of your parents have made real sacrifices this summer in order that you might enjoy camp and have a good time. Maybe they have done some nice little thing, like fixing up your room to surprise you on your return. Don't be afraid to let them know you like it. Oh, maybe it isn't just what you would have chosen; but keep that to yourself. For you do love the thought that made them do it. Mothers can stand an awful lot of loving.

"I'll never forget when I was buying a pair of shoes for one of my daughters. There was one pair I could tell she wanted very much, but it cost two dollars more. She knew that economy in our family was very necessary right then. But I couldn't resist giving her that pleasure, and so we bought the shoes. Never shall I forget the expression of absolute joy on her face, as she jumped up right there in the store and gave me a kiss! She was absolutely unconscious of anybody around her. I must confess, it came as a surprise; but never have I spent two dollars that brought the returns that that did. In a way, it was such a little thing for her to do; but it was such a big thing to me. It will go with me through life. And so, give *your* mothers a little extra appreciation sometimes.

"One of the biggest things that I hope that camp has given to you is friendships; friendships with each other, with the counselors, with Dr. Johnson and with me. And I believe that all you girls will go back to school with a higher ideal of what a boy

friend can be, and what you can be to that boy. Remember how many times I have said that your best times at your age (here I go saying "your age" again) will be had in groups, boys and girls together in work and play. Then you will have learned to know many boys, so that when you are older, you can have one special friend that will really mean something to you. Then will come the time when you should enjoy being with him, and him alone.

"Now, I feel that I must prepare you for some of the disappointments that await you when you get back home. You are all so happy about going home, and that surely does my heart good. You have made up your minds not to let this or that bother you; but some of you won't be home many hours before you find yourselves all tangled up emotionally, and you will feel as if you could scream! Nothing will be going right.

"You may have a little remorse when all is over, but that isn't going to help matters. Pick yourself up, give yourself a little shake, and say to yourself, 'Of course I can't grow up all at once. Of course I shall make mistakes and wish I hadn't; but I am going to try a little harder next time not to let having to wear a silly, ugly old dress get me down. I will talk things over with mother, and I just know everything will be right again.'

"And the boys, oh the boys! They won't make you any too happy either, at times. One boy that was so nice to you before you went away doesn't notice you any more. You begin to feel sorry for yourself. Don't you forget now what I think about you, that you are just wonderful, and that in high school, *one* boy is

Don't you forget now what I think about you, that you are just wonderful, and that in high school, one boy is not what you want anyhow. So look around and find another; and you may like him even better than the first!

not what you want anyhow. So look around and find another–you may like him even better than the first!

"About all your activities. You cannot be kept too busy. Join the school clubs, and work hard to make them succeed. Have fun at your parties; enough so that a parked automobile has little attraction. If you do that, you will get good grades at school, too. You have all dreamed your dreams this summer as to what you'll be some day, and I am counting on all those dreams coming true.

"If I say anything more, I am afraid that lump will come back into my throat. So let's sing the camp song and start packing. It's still early. The busses will leave camp promptly at nine tomorrow morning, and away you will go, laughing and singing. Be good now, and get to sleep early."

The girls broke up and walked off in groups. Mary Ann, Helen and Nell were arm-in-arm planning for the trip back tomorrow. Lady remained by the glowing embers until the last girl was out of sight. She lingered; and there was a prayer in her heart that each one would grow into womanhood fully equipped to make the world a better place, and to create a home that America could be proud of.